SURVIVING D-DAY
TANKS IN NORMANDY

CRAIG MOORE

MILITARY VEHICLES AND ARTILLERY SERIES, VOLUME 2

Front cover image: This impressive-looking M4A1(76) Sherman tank did not land on Utah Beach on D-Day. It arrived later and was used in the beachhead breakout Operation *Cobra*. It was fitted with the long-barreled high-velocity 76mm M1 gun. It is on display outside the Utah Beach D-Day Museum (Le Musée du Débarqué de Utah).

Back cover image: This German Panzer VI Ausf.E Tiger tank is on display by the side of the D979 road just outside Vimoutiers, Normandy, France. On 19 August 1944, it ran out of fuel and had to be abandoned by its crew.

Title page image: This M4A4 Sherman tank hull has been fitted with an M4A3(75)W high-bustle turret from a different tank. It is on display at the Airborne Museum in Sainte-Mère-Église.

Contents page image: Additional appliqué armour slabs were welded on the side of Sherman tanks to offer additional protection for the crew and ammunition. They were not always effective. This tank has a dummy gun and gun mantlet. It was on display at Catz but is undergoing restoration.

Published by Key Books
An imprint of Key Publishing Ltd
PO Box 100
Stamford
Lincs PE19 1XQ

www.keypublishing.com

The right of Craig Moore to be identified as the author of this book has been asserted in accordance with the Copyright, Designs and Patents Act 1988 Sections 77 and 78.

ISBN 978 1 913870 23 2

Acknowledgements
Adrian Barrell, Jack Bennet, Kevin Browne, Pierre-Oliver Buan, Lt Col Colin Bulleid, Lauren Child, Adam Gallon, Nigel Hay, Amber Hopkins, Nick Hopkins, Christopher Jary, Sue Moore, Steve Osfield, Yuri Pasholok, Albert Pujadas, Francis Pulham, Ed Webster and Rick Wedlock.

Typeset by SJmagic DESIGN SERVICES, India.

Contents

Introduction

On 6 June 1944, D-Day, the Allied invasion of northern France began. As part of Operation *Overlord*, around 156,000 Allied soldiers, including 20,000 airborne troops, landed in Normandy on five main beaches: Sword, Juno, Gold, Omaha and Utah. They were supported by thousands of aircraft and ships. Some amphibious Sherman DD tanks swam ashore to provide armoured support for the initial wave of infantry. Most tanks arrived on the beaches by landing craft. A few days later, after the construction of the temporary Mulberry harbour at Arromanches-les-Bains, tanks, supply lorries and more troops started pouring from the ships into the ever-expanding beachhead. Some of the tanks used in the battle, and examples of those tanks that were used later in the war, can still be found in the Normandy countryside or on display in different museums.

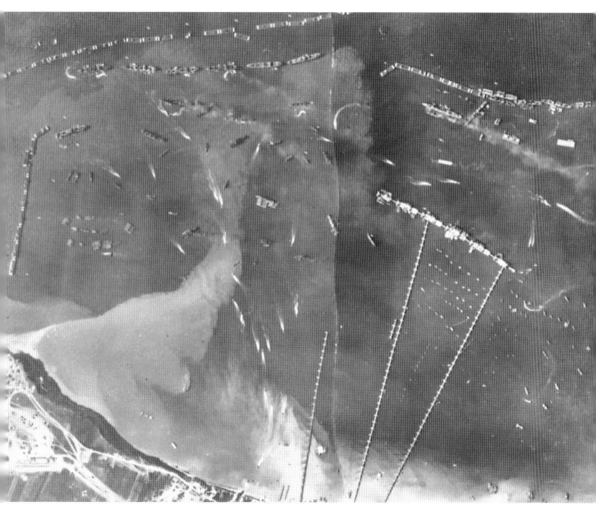

An artificial harbour was constructed at Arromanches to enable supplies, vehicles and troops to be landed in deep water. (Australian War Memorial SUK13282 – Public Domain)

American troops of the 16th Infantry Regiment sheltering from German machine-gun fire and artillery amongst beach obstacles on Omaha Beach during the Normandy D-Day landings on 6 June 1944. (Australian War Memorial P06125.001 – Public Domain)

Omaha Beach today is totally different from how it looked in the Summer of 1944.

If you are going to make a long journey to see a specific tank highlighted in this book, make sure the tank is still there before you go. Tanks move. I know that sounds silly, but preserved surviving tanks used as memorials or museum exhibits are sometimes removed for restoration. On rare occasions, a few are temporarily transported to different locations to be displayed at World War Two anniversary events or used as part of a special exhibition. Send an email to the local tourist board or *mairie* (town hall). An internet search will provide you with the address.

Check opening times before you visit museums. Some close for lunch, others are open only on certain days of the week, and a few open only in the summer.

Although this guidebook is on the surviving tanks in Normandy, it also includes information on two German gun emplacement block houses on Gold Beach. These German beach defence anti-tank guns survived the initial bombing and Navy bombardment. The 88mm anti-tank guns in these reinforced concrete gun emplacements caused havoc on the landing sites as the British started to arrive on the beach. The guns did not point out to sea. Their barrels were aimed along the length of the beach and could fire armour-piercing shells at the side of the Allied tanks trying to drive off the beaches. One was knocked out by a 'Hobart's Funny' Sherman Crab anti-tank mine flail tank. The other was knocked out by a Sexton artillery self-propelled gun firing a shell into the gun aperture, while at the same time another 'Hobart's Funny', a Churchill AVRE, fired a 290mm Petard spigot mortar shell at the rear door at around 3.30pm on D-Day. This is still not common knowledge, which is why these decisive acts of bravery and skill have been included in this book.

This is a French World War One Renault FT tank 'Tobruk' turret used by the Germans as part of the Normandy Atlantic Wall coastal defences. It is on display at the Le Musée du Débarqué de Utah Beach (Utah Beach D-Day Museum).

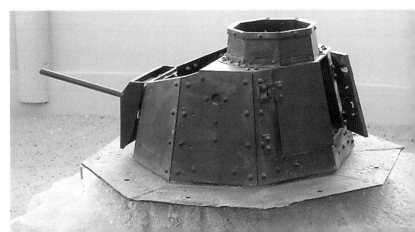

These World War One Renault FT tank turrets were also known as 'Turmstellung' (tower points). The Germans installed them on top of thick concrete bunkers that were usually covered over with earth and grass. The only visible point of this defensive system to an attacking enemy was the small tank turret. It is on display at the Grand Bunker Atlantic Wall Museum, Ouistreham. (Pierre-Olivier Buan)

Not all the tank turrets used in the German Atlantic Wall defences had working guns installed. They were used to provide armoured protection for artillery observers who would radio or phone gun crews, at different points within the network of defensive bunkers, new target locations. This one is on display at the Grand Bunker Atlantic Wall Museum, Ouistreham. (Pierre-Olivier Buan)

Hobart's Funnies

Major Percy Hobart oversaw the development of specially designed vehicles to solve problems that were expected to be encountered during D-Day. The Sherman Crab flail tank cleared paths through mine fields. Churchill AVRE tanks filled anti-tank trenches with fascines and fired 40lb high-explosives

An early prototype Sherman Crab flail tank. (Department of Tank Design report F.T.1016)

mortar shells at fortified strongpoints and beach defences. Sherman Duplex Drive tanks were fitted with inflatable canvas screens that enabled the tanks to swim ashore and support the advancing infantry on the beaches. Churchill AVRE Bobbin tanks unrolled artificial roads across soft sand to prevent following vehicles sinking. Armoured bulldozers and tanks fitted with dozer blades enabled ramps to be built over beach defences. These could also clear obstacles and fill trenches and shell holes as well as help to build roads. The Churchill Crocodile flame-throwing tank was used to attack machine-gun emplacements.

The Churchill Ark Mk.II bridging tank was a turretless Churchill tank with a tracked deck and ramps at the front and rear that could act as a ramp or a bridge. (Fighting Vehicle Proving Establishment report F.T.1584)

The Churchill tank 'Bobbin Carrier' carpet-laying device. A large, wide canvas matting was wound around the reel and unwound on top of soft sand to enable vehicles to drive off the beach. After the carpet was laid, the crews could detach the bobbin from the inside. (Fighting Vehicle Proving Establishment report F.T.1324)

The Churchill Mk.VII tank Crocodile flame thrower was used on D-Day to attack fortified strongpoints. (Australian War Memorial 129596 – Public Domain)

A Sherman M4A2 Duplex Drive amphibious tank prototype with skirts in the down position. (Fighting Vehicle Proving Establishment report FT.1618)

A Sherman M4A2 Duplex Drive amphibious tank prototype with skirts in the up position. (Fighting Vehicle Proving Establishment report FT.1618)

The Sherman M4A2 Duplex Drive amphibious tank prototype was fitted with two propellers at the rear. (Fighting Vehicle Proving Establishment report FT.1618)

The two propellers at the rear of the Sherman M4A2 Duplex Drive amphibious tank are in the down position, ready to start turning. Although the screen has 'MK.2' painted on it, the vehicle was redesignated MK.3. (Fighting Vehicle Proving Establishment report FT.1618)

Waterproofing

Tanks used on the D-Day beaches had to be waterproofed and wading devices fitted to the air-intake vents and exhaust. (Fighting Vehicle Proving Establishment report 7408/1)

Sexton self-propelled artillery guns used on the D-Day beaches also had to be waterproofed and have wading devices fitted to the air-intake vents and exhaust. The sides of the fighting compartment had to be temporarily raised. (Fighting Vehicle Proving Establishment report 7266/4)

Tanks used on D-Day had their gun mantlets, hatch joints and openings waterproofed before they were loaded onto tank landing craft. (Fighting Vehicle Proving Establishment report 6458/1)

Stuart light tanks used on the D-Day beaches were also waterproofed and had wading devices fitted to the air-intake vents and exhaust. (Fighting Vehicle Proving Establishment report FT 1543)

East Normandy Sites

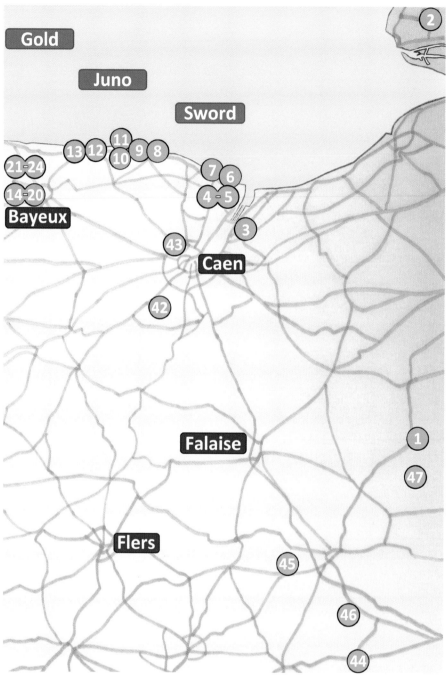

To plan your exploration of Normandy, so that it includes visiting as many of the surviving tanks as possible, use these sketch maps. The green circles show the location of surviving tanks on display in Normandy. The numbers indicate the chapter that provides information about that tank. Two merged green circles indicate that there is more than one tank at the location, which is usually a museum. The following chapter numbers are shown as a range: 4–5, 14–20, 21–24, 26–32.

West Normandy Sites

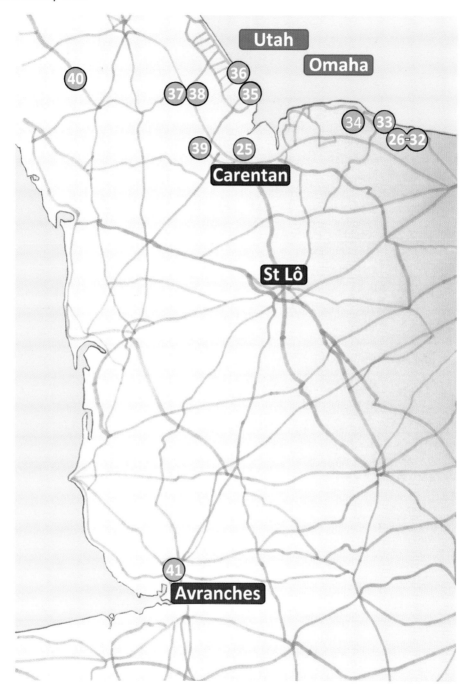

Chapter 1

Tiger Tank
Vimoutiers

Location: Set your navigation device to Vimoutiers, Avenue du Maréchal Leclerc. This is the D979. When your device says you have arrived, drive east out of town uphill. The Vimoutiers Tiger tank is about a mile outside of the town in a lay-by. This stretch of the D979 road does not have a name.

On 19 August 1944, several German tanks, including the Vimoutiers Tiger, were making their way to get refuelled at an Army fuel dump. They had to make a detour along the Vimoutiers–Gace road to escape the encirclement of the Falaise pocket. The Vitmoutiers Tiger ran out of fuel and ground to a halt in the middle of the road. The crew placed the demolition charges they had been given on the engine cover and turret. The explosives caused the armoured covers on top of the engine to buckle. The turret was jammed by the second explosion.

A U.S. Army bulldozer was used to push it off the road to enable the essential supply lorries to reach the ever-moving front. French scrap-metal merchant Morat purchased the salvage rights to scrap the Tiger tank. He took out the transmission but left the tank sitting on the northern side of the road in a ditch, with its gun pointing menacingly up the road at passing vehicles. For over 30 years it was left to rust and get covered in moss. Local children would play on this once deadly weapon of war. It became a local landmark. Mr Morat's sister inherited the Tiger tank when he died. She did not want it and sold it to a scrap-metal merchant in Caen. It was too heavy to be towed away, and the company arrived on site with oxyacetylene metal-cutting tools to cut it up piece by piece and transport it away to a smelter in Caen.

A local resident saw what was happening to the town's historic landmark and was horrified. He contacted the Mayor of Vimoutiers, who obtained an emergency purchase order for the tank on behalf of the town of Vimoutiers, authorised by the Paris War Office. In October 1975, the work of restoring the Tiger tank began with its removal from the roadside ditch. All the hatches were welded shut. It does not have an engine or a gearbox. There are lots of external and internal parts missing. The most noticeable external parts are the upper track guards and the rear twin exhausts.

Specifications	
Length:	8.45m
Width:	3.70m
Height:	3.00m
Weight:	57 tonnes
Engine:	Maybach HL 210 P45 V12 690hp
Crew:	5
Main gun:	8.8cm Kw.K.36 L/56
Other weapons:	Two 7.92mm MG34 machine guns
Armour:	15mm–100mm
Sustained road speed:	25mph
Max. range on roads:	110 miles
Total built:	1,345

Chapter 2

Churchill Mk.VII Tank
Fontaine-la-Mallet, Le Havre

Location: Fontaine-la-Mallet, Route de Fontaine-la-Mallet (D52) junction with Rue Roger Stil.

This British Churchill Mk.VII tank forms the major part of a war memorial to all the soldiers who lost their lives during Operation *Astonia*, the capture of the German-held port of Le Havre on 10 September 1944.

The Churchill Mk.VII tank was restored and donated by the Tank Museum, Bovington, England. Churchill tanks were used in the attack on Le Havre. It was previously a gate guardian at the Queen's Own Yeomanry Dale Barracks, Chester, UK. It has a dummy barrel. The War Department T number on the side of the tank is wrong.

Operation *Astonia* began on 10 September 1944. The 49th West Riding Infantry (Polar Bears) attacked in the east. The 51st Highland Division advanced on the west. They were supported by three armoured brigades, artillery and some 'Hobart's Funnies' from the 79th Armoured Division. About 4,500 Allied soldiers took part. The Germans had approximately 11,000 men entrenched in different defences. Between 4.15pm and 5.45pm, Allied bombers dropped 4,720 tons of bombs. At 5.45pm the assault began from the north, half a mile from the memorial. The Allies used flails to clear minefields and assault bridges to cross anti-tank ditches. The first strongpoints were reached at 7.22pm, with heavy losses. At midnight, the second phase of Operation *Astonia* began in an attack towards Fontaine-la-Mallet. At 5.30am on 11 September 1944, the attack headed from Gainneville to Le Havre.

The shelling from the massed artillery was unrelenting on the German troops defending the port. On 12 September 1944, when Fort de Tourneville, Le Havre, was also threatened by the tanks of the 7th Royal Tank Regiment, the German commander Oberst Wildermuth, wounded and in pyjamas (which nevertheless bore his medals) surrendered the garrison.

The vital port of Le Havre was now in the hands of the Allies, but the destruction wrought upon the port by both the Allied bombardment and by the German demolition crews who tried to make the dock unusable meant that the port was not back in operation until 9 October 1944. The Allies reported just under 500 killed, wounded or missing.

Specifications	
Length:	7.36m
Width:	2.87m
Height:	2.61m
Weight:	39.5 tons
Engine:	Bedford 12-cylinder, water-cooled, horizontally opposed, L-head 350hp petrol engine
Crew:	5
Main gun:	Ordnance QF 75mm
Other weapons:	Two 7.92mm Besa machine guns
Armour:	16mm–152mm
Sustained road speed:	13.5mph
Max. range on roads:	142 miles
Total built:	1,400

Chapter 3

Centaur IV CS Tank
Pegasus Bridge Memorial Museum, Ranville

Location: Ranville 14860, Avenue du Major Howard (or Ranville 14860, Impasse Pegasus).

The Centaur was designed to provide close support to the Royal Marines landing on the French coast of Normandy on D-Day, 6 June 1944. The 95mm howitzer gun was intended to be fired from the landing craft at enemy fortifications on the beach. The compass-like turret markings allowed the battery commander outside the tanks to direct all the tank howitzers to the correct location on the beach. This restored Royal Marines Close Support Centaur Mark IV tank used to sit opposite the Pegasus Bridge Café next to the canal and the bridge, but it has now been moved to the grounds of the Pegasus Bridge Memorial Museum on the other side of the canal along with the original bridge. This Mark IV Centaur was built by Leyland. It was part of V Troop of the 5th Independent Battery of the Royal Marines Armoured Support Group (RMASG), and it landed on D-Day at Sword Beach between La Brèche d'Hermanville and Lion-sur-Mer. The tank came into contact with the enemy 500 yards past the beach. It reversed up to a hedge but was hit by mortar fire that set the bins and then the engine compartment on fire. The crew evacuated the Centaur. It was left behind as the fighting moved on.

The tank was recovered in 1975 from Hermanville, then restored by 60 Station Workshop, REME, in Antwerp and put on display in June 1977. Most of the Centaur's road wheels, as well as some other parts, are not original. With the opening of the new Pegasus Bridge Memorial Museum, the tank underwent a full restoration in 2014 and found a new home in the grounds of the museum.

The Royal Marines Armoured Support Group saw action on D-Day. It was equipped with 20 Shermans and 80 Centaur Mark IV close-support tanks. Within 15 minutes of H-Hour, 20 Centaurs were ashore, and eight more followed within four hours. They were intended only to operate during the initial assault and within one mile of the beach, but they stayed in action for 15 days and as much as 10 miles inland.

Specifications	
Length:	6.35m
Width:	2.44m
Height:	2.88m
Weight:	27 tons
Engine:	Nuffield Liberty V12 410hp petrol engine
Crew:	5
Main gun:	Royal Ordnance QF 95mm howitzer
Other weapons:	Two 7.92mm Besa machine guns
Armour:	20mm–76mm
Sustained road speed:	24mph
Max. range on roads:	165 miles
Total built:	80 issued to Royal Marine Armoured Support Group

Chapter 4

105mm Howitzer Motor Carriage M7 Priest SPG
Ouistreham

Location: Ouistreham 14150, Avenue du 6 Juin, junction with Avenue de la Plage. Le Grand Bunker, Musée du Mur de l'Atlantique.

This 105mm Howitzer Gun Motor Carriage M7 is believed to come from the Commes collection. The British called it '105mm Self-Propelled Gun, Priest', due to the armoured pulpit-like observation tower. It was one of three recovered from the seabed in 1988. They were on an LCT (Landing Craft Tank) that sank as it approached the Normandy beaches on D-Day 6 June 1944, three miles off Port-en-Bessin. This one is on display at Le Grand Bunker, Musée du Mur de l'Atlantique, which is set back from the coast. It was a German observation tower that was part of the Atlantic wall defences. It was also used as an ammunition store, command and control centre for the defence of the Orne River estuary, first-aid post, telephone operation centre and radio transmission post.

Ouistreham is an attractive seaside port that became a battlefield when the British, French and Commonwealth troops landed at Sword Beach, Normandy, on D-Day. Other 105mm M7s were successfully landed ashore on D-Day. The artillery regiments of the British 3rd and 50th Divisions and the Canadian 3rd Division were equipped with the Priest. British and Canadian units started replacing their Priests with 25pdr Sexton artillery self-propelled guns and towed 25pdr guns, shortly after D-Day. This helped ease supply problems and reduced the reliance on U.S. Army logistics shipping 105mm shells to their allies. The British supply chain, in the early days of the invasion of France, now only had to transport one type of large artillery high-explosive shell rather than two.

Photographs show that the British and Commonwealth Priests in Normandy were fitted with three-piece final-drive housings. They had either the early or the later style heavy-duty bogies. Many, if not all, were equipped with additional protective armour on the hull sides. The first Priests off the landing crafts were waterproofed and fitted with extra metal side and rear plates to prevent waves crashing over the vehicle and flooding it as the vehicle crawled out of the sea and onto the beach. The air intake and exhausts had large temporary metal snorkels fitted to stop water ingress. These were discarded as soon as possible.

Specifications	
Length:	6.01m
Width:	2.87m
Height:	2.94m
Weight:	22.58 tons
Engine:	Continental R975 C1 radial 9-cylinder 340hp petrol engine
Crew:	7
Main gun:	105mm M2A1 howitzer
Other weapons:	0.50cal (12.7mm) MG HB M2 Browning machine gun
Armour:	12.7mm–50.8mm
Sustained road speed:	21mph
Max. range on roads:	120 miles
Total built:	3,490

Chapter 5

M3A3 Stuart Tank
The Grand Bunker Atlantic Wall Museum, Ouistreham

Location: Ouistreham 14150, Avenue du 6 Juin, junction with Avenue de la Plage. Le Grand Bunker, Musée du Mur de l'Atlantique.

You can tell the difference between an M3A3 Stuart and an M5 Stuart by looking at the engine hatch covers. In this M3A3 tank at Ouistreham's Le Grand Bunker Museum, they are flat and in line with the rest of the hull top. The engine hatch covers on the back of the M5 Stuart are raised. It is on loan from the Musée des Blindés (The Armour Museum), Saumur, France. For many years it carried the markings of an M3A3 Stuart light tank belonging to the reconnaissance troop 27th Armoured Brigade. It displayed the 27th Armoured Brigade yellow and white seahorse on a blue shield tactical identification badge on the front and rear of the hull along with a white number 50 painted on a red square and a red diamond symbol on the side to show it was part of the Brigade Headquarters. It would have a red number with a white border on the side of the turret, normally in the range of 1 to 11. The black number 14 in the yellow circle should be a 16; it was the weight limit for bridge crossing. This tank weighed 14.46 tons. In 2012 it was repainted. It would have had a white star on the roof for aerial recognition.

Surprisingly, this small tank had a four-man crew: a commander, gunner, driver and co-driver/machine gunner. It was very cramped. It was powered by a Continental W-670-9A 7-cylinder air-cooled radial engine that produced 250hp. It gave the Stuart a maximum road speed of 31mph (50km/h), and off-road it could go at 18mph (29km/h). It did not have room for large fuel tanks, so it only had an operational road range of about 135 miles (217km) before it needed to be refuelled.

The M3A3 Stuart light tank was meant to be used as a reconnaissance scout vehicle and not to engage enemy tanks in combat. The British and Commonwealth troops also called these light tanks 'Honeys' because they were a 'sweet' and easy drive.

Specifications	
Length:	5.02m
Width:	2.52m
Height:	2.56m
Weight:	14.46 tons
Engine:	Continental W-670-9A 7-cylinder 250hp petrol engine
Crew:	4
Main gun:	37mm M6 gun
Other weapons:	Two .30 cal. Browning M1919A4 machine guns; one .30 cal. Browning M1919A5 machine gun
Armour:	9.5mm–51mm
Sustained road speed:	31mph
Max. range on roads:	135 miles
Total built:	3,427

Chapter 6

Centaur IV CS Tank
Hermanville-sur-Mer

Location: Hermanville-sur-Mer 14880, Avenue Félix Faure at the junction with Rue du Dr Turgis.

The tank has been painted to look like a Royal Marines Armoured Support Group British Centaur IV Close Support Tank. The Centaur tank was very similar to the Cromwell tank except it had different suspension, a less powerful engine and a Royal Ordnance QF 95mm L/18 howitzer artillery gun instead of the Cromwell's 75mm anti-tank gun. They were used on D-Day to fire on German beach defences from tank landing craft. It would have originally been painted either brown or green. The compass-like turret markings allowed the battery commander outside the tanks to direct all the tank howitzers to the correct location of the next target on the beach.

At 8am on D-Day, commandos were landed on Queen Red Sector of Sword Beach facing La Breche. Troop 1 and Troop 8 were composed of French commandos led by Captain Frigate Kieffer whose task was to capture Ouistreham, supported by tanks of the 5th Royal Marine Independent Armoured Support Battery and elements of No. 4 Commando. The Germans resisted, but a British Centaur IV tank helped silence the opposing defences with its 95mm high-explosive shells.

This tank was originally a turretless Centaur Dozer that had been converted from tank hulls built for the cancelled Anti-Aircraft Centaur tank programme. It had a large bulldozer blade fixed to the front of the tank. The armoured dozers were built to push debris, concrete blocks and knocked-out tanks and vehicles off the road so the Allied advance inland could continue on D-Day while keeping the crew safe from small-arms fire.

It was converted to look like a Centaur Close Support Tank to honour the role played by the Royal Marines in the attack on Sword Beach on D-Day. The coastal seaside resort of Hermanville-sur-Mer was part of the British Sector, Sword Beach. It was restored and modified at the Imperial War Museum, Duxford, workshops and fitted with a Cavalier turret that had been recovered from the Otterburn firing range in England. Some of the fittings from when it was used as a Centaur Dozer can still be seen on the hull.

Specifications	
Length:	6.35m
Width:	2.44m
Height:	2.88m
Weight:	27 tons
Engine:	Nuffield Liberty V12 410hp petrol engine
Crew:	5
Main gun:	Royal Ordnance QF 95mm L/18 howitzer
Other weapons:	Two 0.303in (7.92mm) Besa machine guns
Armour:	20mm–76mm
Sustained road speed:	24mph
Max. range on roads:	165 miles
Total built:	80 issued to Royal Marine Armoured Support Group

Chapter 7

Churchill Mk.IV AVRE Tank
Lion-sur-Mer

Location: Lion-sur-Mer 14780, Boulevard Anatole France at the junction with Avenue de Blagny.

This Churchill Mk.IV AVRE (Armoured Vehicles Royal Engineers) tank was armed with a Petard 290mm spigot mortar that was designed to blow up concrete fortifications, fortified houses, destroy concrete sea walls and beach defences. It could fire a 40lb (18kg) high-explosive warhead 150 yards (137m). The gun was not loaded inside the tank. Where the gun meets the turret, there is a hinge. It was the tank's co-driver who reloaded the 290mm spigot mortar by staying in his hatch, with the turret gun over his position, and the short mortar tube was bent downwards. The new mortar shell was then inserted into the front of the gun. The hinge was then moved up so the mortar tube was now back in the horizontal position. The co-driver's and driver's hatches were enlarged to enable the weapon to be reloaded more easily. This tank has the classic Churchill tank ribbed 'catwalk' upper track guard. The Churchill AVRE at Graye-sur-Mer has a smooth metal upper track guard.

This tank memorial was the idea of General Sir Ian Harris who commanded the 2nd R.U.R. (Royal Ulster Rifles) infantry battalion on D-Day. On this western end of Sword Beach, Lieutenant-Colonel Gray and his men of 41st Commandos were met with accurate fire from the moment they set foot on land. Besides their human casualties, they found themselves with no radio until the afternoon and were bombed by the Luftwaffe the following morning. Elements of the German 21st Panzer Division slipped between the British 3rd Division and Canadian 3rd Division. The Allied combat troops on 'Sword' and 'Juno' beaches had not linked up at that stage. The Allied beachhead was under threat. At 8pm, the Germans reached the French seaside towns of Luc-sur-Mer and Lion-sur-Mer. The Germans were not reinforced and had to withdraw. They had seen the English Channel for the last time. The survivors of 41st Commando were reinforced by the Royal Lincolnshire Regiment and the Royal Ulster Rifles. They then went back on the attack and liberated Lion-sur-Mer, then marched on to liberate Luc-sur-Mer. This tank previously stood as a memorial at the entrance to La Breche beach.

Specifications	
Length:	7.34m
Width:	2.87m
Height:	2.49m
Weight:	38.5 tons
Engine:	Bedford 12-cylinder, water-cooled, horizontally opposed, L-head 350hp petrol engine
Crew:	5
Main gun:	Petard 290mm spigot mortar
Other weapons:	Two 7.92mm Besa machine guns
Armour:	16mm–89mm
Sustained road speed:	16.4mph (max road speed: 17.3mph)
Max. range on roads:	123 miles
Total built:	564

Chapter 8

M4A4(75) Sherman V DD Tank
Courseulles-sur-Mer

Location: Courseulles-sur-Mer 14470, Quai des Allies junction with Place du 6 Juin.

The British and Commonwealth armies did not use the same naming system as that used by the Americans. This is a Sherman V DD (Duplex-Drive) tank. The U.S. Army designation for this type of Sherman tank is M4A4(75). What is fascinating about this tank is that the boat-shaped frame for the canvas skirt of the DD is still attached to the tank's hull. The rear propellers have been removed, but the transmission gears can still be seen at the back of the tank near the rear engine compartment access doors. Its hull is covered with military plaques that commemorate the military units that landed on this section of the D-Day coast.

The Sherman V tank first saw combat with the 12th Canadian Tank Regiment in an assault landing at Pachino Bay in Sicily on 10 July 1943. Sherman V tanks were assigned to British and Commonwealth tank regiments under the lend-lease agreement. They made up the bulk of the Commonwealth 75mm Sherman tanks used in Normandy. Unlike the American DD tanks that were released into the sea too far out from the beach in rough seas, most of the British and Commonwealth DD tanks made it to shore.

The planning started in 1943 for the launching of a massive invasion on the French coast. Everyone knew that it was going to be a very difficult operation to land thousands of men and equipment from the sea onto a beach under heavy fire. The troops landing on the beaches would need tank support – fast. The idea of making tanks swim ashore was suggested. The engineers came up with the Sherman Duplex-Drive tanks.

The planners' worry was that if the tank landing craft all got hit by the coastal defence guns, the troops would be without tank support. Independent swimming tanks spread the risk of losses. The tanks would slip into the water a few miles out to sea and head towards the shore. Each tank would be a smaller target to hit. The idea behind Duplex-Drive tanks was the science of displacement. If you can push out enough water, roughly 33 tons of water – nearly the same weight of the Sherman tank – then the tank will float. Propellers were added at the back of the tank to propel the tank to shore at around 3mph. Once the tank was on the beach, the canvas screen would be collapsed, and the tank would be able to engage enemy targets.

Specifications	
Length:	6.05m
Width:	2.61m
Height:	2.74m
Weight:	31.11 tons
Engine:	Chrysler A57 30-cylinder, 4-cycle, multibank 425hp petrol engine
Crew:	5
Main gun:	75mm gun M3 in an M34 mount
Other weapons:	Two .30cal MG M1919A4 machine guns; one .50cal MG HB M2 machine gun
Armour:	12.7mm–76.2mm
Sustained road speed:	20mph
Max. range on roads:	100 miles
Total built:	7,499

Chapter 9

Churchill Mk.IV AVRE Tank
Graye-sur-Mer

Location: Courseulles-sur-Mer 14470, Voie des Français Libres at the junction with Avenue du Général de Gaulle.

This obstacle-clearance Churchill Mk.IV AVRE (Armoured Vehicle Royal Engineers) tank belonged to the British 26th Engineer Squadron. On 6 June 1944, very early in the morning, it drove off an LCT, onto the beach, but then sank into a 4m-deep bomb crater, concealed from its driver by the shallow flooded area that surrounded it. Four members of its six-man crew were killed by German machine-gun and rifle fire as they tried to escape. The other two were seriously injured and had to be evacuated later in the day.

A bridge was built over the sunken Churchill tank to allow Allied troops across the flooded land. The tank was used as the bridge support. It remained buried for 32 years. In November 1976, a team of British Army soldiers and engineers extracted the Churchill AVRE tank from its wartime grave. It was restored in the French Army workshops in Caen, and then erected on a concrete plinth by the beach exit, as a memorial to all the brave soldiers who had died or were wounded on Juno Beach on D-Day. It is situated only a few metres from where it had sunk into the large flooded bomb hole. When the driver of this tank, Bill Dunn, died in 2014, in accordance with his last wishes, on 8 November 2014 his ashes were scattered next to his tank. There is a small plaque that commemorates this by the side of the tank on a large stone.

This tank was armed with a Petard 290mm spigot mortar. It was used to knock out 'Atlantic Wall' beach defences. It could fire a 40lb (18kg) high-explosive warhead 150 yards (137m). The gun was not loaded inside the tank. Where the gun meets the turret, there is a hinge. It was the tank's co-driver who reloaded the 290mm spigot mortar by staying in his hatch, with the turret gun over his position, and the short mortar tube was bent downwards. The new mortar shell was then inserted into the front of the gun. The hinge was then moved up, so the mortar tube was now back in the horizontal position.

Specifications	
Length:	7.34m
Width:	2.87m
Height:	2.49m
Weight:	38.5 tons
Engine:	Bedford 12-cylinder, water-cooled, horizontally opposed, L-head 350hp petrol engine
Crew:	5
Main gun:	Petard 290mm spigot mortar
Other weapons:	Two 7.92mm Besa machine guns
Armour:	16mm–89mm
Sustained road speed:	16.4mph (max. road speed: 17.3mph)
Max. range on roads:	123 miles
Total built:	564

Chapter 10

25pdr Sexton Self-Propelled Artillery Gun
Ver-sur-Mer

Location: Ver-sur-Mer 14114, Route d'Asnelles junction with Avenue du 6 Juin.

The memorial square is called 'Espace Robert Kiln' in honour of Major Robert Kiln, who took part in the D-Day landings with the 86th Field Regiment Royal Artillery on Gold Beach, 'K' for King Sector. This 25-pounder Sexton self-propelled artillery gun was presented to the town of Ver-sur-Mer by the major's son, Dr Mathew Kiln, in memory of his father and all the British troops who landed on Gold Beach on 6 June 1944 and the days that followed.

The 86th (Hertfordshire Yeomanry) Field Regiment, Royal Artillery, was a Territorial (part-time volunteer reserve) unit which mobilised with towed guns in 1939 and converted to self-propelled artillery guns in 1943. Their guns engaged enemy targets at La Riviere from their landing craft as they approached King Sector, Gold Beach, 35 minutes before H-hour (H-35) at a range of more than 12,000 yards (11,000m). They continued firing at four rounds a minute until H-7, when fire was transferred to the heavily fortified area around the lighthouse for a further 20 minutes.

The landing craft then turned around and waited a short distance out to sea until called back to the beach. The first three troops unloaded 12 guns and started firing from Gold Beach soon after 8.30am. Forward artillery observers from the regiment – who were with the leading infantry, now some 3 miles (5km) inland – directed supporting fire onto German defences.

Behind the Sexton is a Porpoise ammunition tank sledge. This is a very rare piece of military equipment that has survived the D-Day beach clear-ups. The D-Day planners were concerned that tanks and self-propelled artillery guns like the Sexton, which landed in the first assault wave of fierce fighting, might run out of ammunition. This led to the idea that they could bring additional supplies ashore in a towed armoured container. Reserve stocks would then be available long before it was safe for wheeled ammunition lorries to land on the beaches. By April 1944 it had been decided that assaulting tanks would drag their extra ammunition ashore in a sealed, submersible container, for all practical purposes a sledge, which was given the name 'Porpoise'.

There were two models: the larger one was capable of carrying approximately the same amount of ammunition, for main armament and machine guns, as could be stowed inside the tank. This doubled the firing capacity of the Sherman tank. Self-propelled artillery units, both field and anti-tank, were also equipped with Porpoise sledges to increase the amount of ammunition available in the early stages of the battle. The one on display at Ver-sur-Mer is the No.2 Porpoise, which was the larger version. (For specifications, see Chapter 17.)

Chapter 11

Gun Emplacement Wn.33
Boulevard de la Plage, Ver-sur-Mer, Gold Beach

Location: Ver-sur-Mer, Boulevard de la Plage, junction with Avenue Marguerite Montrouge.

On D-Day, trooper Jim Smith of B Squadron, Westminster Dragoons, was a gunner in a Sherman Crab tank fitted with an anti-mine flail device on a 10ft boom at the front. His gun was pointed to the rear of the tank as they approached Gold Beach near La Reverie, in an LCT. This would prevent the barrel from getting caked in sand and mud, as the chains on the circular boom arms started to pound the ground to explode any buried German mines. At about 7.25am the landing craft ramp went down, and two 82 Squadron, 6 Assault Regiment, Royal Engineers, Churchill AVRE tanks drove off onto the sand. There were two large explosions. Both tanks were hit in the side by armour-piercing shells fired from a German beach defence 8.8cm Pak 43/41 anti-tank gun situated in a concrete casemate, numbered Wn.33. This gun emplacement had survived the initial bombing and shelling. Its gun pointed along the length of the beach, not out to sea.

The gun crew had never seen a Sherman Crab before. It must have appeared to them to be less of a threat compared with the other tanks starting to land further down the shoreline. They turned their attention to them. This gave Jim Smith the chance to turn his gun towards the German bunker. He fired two high-explosive shells at the gun aperture, but the German gun kept firing down the beach. He then loaded an armour-piercing round and fired it at the enemy gun. It went straight through the aperture and knocked out the gun, enabling other tanks to land on this section of Gold Beach.

The British Army first used mine clearance flail tanks in the deserts of North Africa in 1942. The design was modified and went into production to be ready in time for D-Day. The Sherman tank was chosen to have a permanently mounted flail system fitted. The Sherman Crab's flail was powered by the tank's engine. The rotor was fitted with 43 long chains that were spun at 142rpm. This speed could be altered when the tank slowed down to clear an obstacle or go uphill. If an exploding mine damaged a chain, a new one could be added later. Cutter blades were added to the rotor. These cut barbed wire and stopped the flail from getting entangled. An armoured blast shield between the flail chains and the front of the tank helped protect the crew from the effects of mine detonation. Unfortunately, there is no surviving example of a Sherman Crab in Normandy.

Opposite above: Shells fired from the German beach defence anti-tank gun situated in this concrete brick casemate, No. Wn.33, could fire along the west beach.(© Jack Beckett)

Opposite below: The anti-tank gun situated on this side of the concrete brick casemate, No. Wn.33, could fire the length of the east beach and hit the flanks of tanks driving onto the beach from tank landing craft.(© Jack Beckett)

Left: M4A4(75) Sherman Crab anti-mine flail tank on display at the National War and Resistance Museum, Overloon, The Netherlands. There are no surviving examples of this tank in Normandy.

Chapter 12

Gun Emplacement Wn.37
Boulevard de la Mer, Asnelles-sur-Mer, Gold Beach

Location: Asnelles-sur-Mer 14960, Boulevard de la Mer, junction with Rue Xavier d'Anselme.

Gold Beach was the central beach of the five designated landing beaches on D-Day. It was more than 10 miles wide and ran from Port-en-Bessin to Ver-sur-Mer. Only certain parts of it were attacked. When the first wave of British Churchill AVRE, Centaur and Sherman Crab tanks landed on the Jig-Green section of Gold Beach, east of Le Hamel, many were knocked out by an 8.8cm Pak 43/41 anti-tank gun situated in a type 677 concrete casemate, numbered Wn.37. It had a clear field of fire down the beach. The coastal defences at 'Le Hamel East' had been missed by the initial bombardment from the sea and bombing from the air. This caused problems. The DD Sherman swimming tanks of the second assault wave tried to destroy the gun with their 14-pound, 75mm high-explosive shells, but failed. Most of them were knocked out and littered the beach. The enemy gun was also damaging landing craft. A few 25pdr Sexton artillery self-propelled guns on the next wave were also knocked out, but several made it up the beach and past the sand dunes along with some other tanks and infantry.

The Hampshire Regiment's objective was the defences at 'Le Hamel East', but the strong longshore drift current had pushed their infantry landing craft east. They landed opposite the gun emplacement Wn.36. Despite being fired upon by the soldiers manning the gun emplacement Wn.37 at 'Le Hamel East', they managed to overcome the German defenders in Wn.36 as they were groggy from the after-effects of the successful early morning bombardment at this location. Company A of the 1st Battalion, Hampshire Regiment, 231st Brigade, then moved west along Gold Beach to attack their primary objective, the coastal defences Wn.37 at 'Le Hamel East'. The attack came to a halt as they came under heavy fire. It was decided to stop the beach attack and mount a new attack from inland.

Company B of the Hampshire Regiment, with help from a Churchill AVRE tank called 'Loch Leven', commanded by Sergeant Bert Scaife RE, circled around Asnelles-sur-Mer (pronounced 'an-ell') and headed back north towards the coast at Le Hamel. The tank crew fired two 290mm Petard spigot 40lb mortar rounds, each containing a 25lb high-explosive warhead, at the old sanitorium hospital that had been converted into a sniper and machine-gun-infested strongpoint. The defenders surrendered. The Churchill AVRE tank then got close to the back of the gun emplacement and fired another 290mm Petard spigot mortar round at the back door.

At the same time, Sergeant Robert E. Palmer of the 147th (Essex Yeomanry) Field Regiment Royal Artillery, who commanded a 25pdr Sexton artillery self-propelled gun called 'Foxholes', attacked the front of the gun emplacement. A Sexton only had thin armour and was not intended to be used as a front-line assault weapon. They got within 300 yards (274m) of the location by driving towards the coast from inland, along a line of trees. He instructed the driver to turn a sharp 45 degrees as soon as they passed the last bit of cover and the gunner to open fire. Two 25lb high-explosive shells were fired at the gun aperture. The second one went in and exploded. The attack from the front and the rear put the gun out of action. This happened at around 3.30pm. Some of the defenders survived. Most were German, but a few were shouting, 'Russkis! Russkis!' as they surrendered. These enemy soldiers had fought with determination and courage, holding up the beach landings for nearly eight hours. They were told the 21st Panzer Division was fighting its way to the beaches. The successful attacks by the Sexton, Churchill AVRE and men of the Hampshire Regiment allowed the 231st Infantry Brigade to continue their advance inland. Sergeant Palmer was awarded the Military Medal, and Sergeant Bert Scaife received the Distinguished Conduct Medal, for their actions on D-Day.

The German 8.8cm Pak 43/41 anti-tank gun crew fired their weapon out of this, now boarded up, aperture. The fortified sanitorium hospital was directly behind the gun emplacement. It was demolished after the war.

This is the clear, unobstructed view the Hamel East German 8.8cm Pak 43/41 anti-tank gun crew in casemate Wn.37 had of the Jig-Green section of Gold Beach on D-Day.

Chapter 13

M4A2(75) Sherman III Tank
Arromanches-les-Bains

Location: Arromanches-les-Bains 14177, Rue Charles Laurent at the junction with Rue Lucien Joly.

British and Commonwealth forces called this tank the Sherman III. The U.S. Army designation for the tank was M4A2(75) Medium Tank, Sherman. It is a World War Two memorial to all the men who fought on Gold Beach in and around Arromanches-les-Bains on and after 6 June 1944. It was used by the French Army after the war. Most visitors fail to notice that it is parked on top of a German gun emplacement that was part of the Atlantic Wall defences.

The Allies had planned to use the Normandy seaside resort of Arromanches-les-Bains as its major supply port. They towed large concrete harbour walls to this area of the coast and constructed an artificial harbour. Old ships were scuttled nearby to create a sea wall to provide shelter from storms. The Allies wanted the road network behind the town and most of its streets to remain damage-free so supply lorries and tanks could advance inland without any problem. For this reason, the town was not heavily bombed and shelled. The 1st Battalion of the Hampshire Regiment was given the task of capturing Arromanches-les-Bains, not by direct assault from the sea but by landing in Asnelles and marching westward to engage the enemy defences from inland. The German defenders were finally overpowered at 10.30pm on 6 June 1944.

The M4A2 Sherman tank's main gun was the standard 75mm medium-velocity general-purpose gun. It could fire high-explosive shells as well as armour-piercing rounds. Although the gun could knock out Panzer III and IV tanks, it had difficulty penetrating the frontal armour of the Panther and Tiger tanks the Allies encountered in the Normandy breakout. It also had two .30cal Browning M1919A4 machine guns: one fitted in the hull and another next to the main gun in the turret. Armour thickness ranged from 12.7mm to 88.9mm. Additional metal plates were welded onto the side of M4A2 Sherman tanks to try to help protect the driver and co-driver, and the ammunition stowage area.

Specifications	
Length:	5.91m
Width:	2.61m
Height:	2.74m
Weight:	31.33 tons
Engine:	General Motors 6046 12-cylinder, 2-cycle, twin in-line, 410hp diesel engine
Crew:	5
Main gun:	75mm gun M3 in an M34A1 mount
Other weapons:	Two .30cal MG M1919A4 machine guns; one .50cal MG HB M2 machine gun; 2in mortar M3 (smoke)
Armour:	12.7mm–88.9mm
Sustained road speed:	25mph
Max. range on roads:	150 miles
Total built:	8,053

Chapter 14

Churchill Mk.VII Crocodile Flamethrower Tank
Bayeux

Location: Bayeux 14400, Boulevard Fabien Ware.

This Churchill Mk VII Flamethrower Tank is on display at the Battle of Normandy Memorial Museum (le Musée Mémorial de la Bataille de Normandie) near the large Bayeux War Cemetery. The D5 Boulevard Fabien Ware is part of the ring road around Bayeux built by the British Royal Engineers in June to enable the troops, tanks and supply vehicles to get to the battlefront quickly and to avoid having to struggle through the narrow streets of the city of Bayeux. Be aware that the museum closes for lunch. You can still see the tanks as they are outside, even if the museum is closed.

They were not called 'Crocodiles' because of the way the tank moved when the flamethrower 400gal fuel trailer was attached to the back of the vehicle, even though it seemed to waddle side to side very slowly just like a big crocodile on dry land. The British and Canadians used names of aggressive wildlife (real and mythical) for their flamethrower mounts and systems – not the vehicles – including the 'Wasp', 'Adder', 'Badger', 'Basilisk', 'Cockatrice' and 'Crocodile'. The Crocodile was feared by the German troops. The mere sound of the Churchill tank jetting flame out of its hull nozzle was enough sometimes to get the occupants of a gun emplacement or fortified house to surrender.

The 75mm gun barrel of this Churchill Mk VII Flamethrower Tank shows evidence of having been cut in half and not accurately rejoined. The tank was manufactured in September 1943. It was recovered from the compound of Pounds Shipowners and Shipbreakers Ltd at Tipnor, Portsmouth, England. It was cleaned and stripped of its badly rusted track guards and stowage boxes.

Prime Minister Margaret Thatcher presented this Churchill Mk VII Crocodile flamethrower, on behalf of the British nation, to the inhabitants of Normandy, in commemoration of the Franco–British co-operation during the liberation of France in 1944. The tank name 'Ashforder' is painted on the air-intake covers near the A-tank War Department T-number T17325837. That number is wrong, as it is too long and should only have six digits.

Specifications	
Length:	7.36m
Width:	2.87m
Height:	2.61m
Weight:	39.5 tons
Engine:	Bedford 12-cylinder, water-cooled, horizontally opposed, L-head 350hp petrol engine
Crew:	5
Main gun:	Royal Ordnance QF 75mm
Other weapons:	One flame thrower in a Crocodile mount; one 7.92mm Besa machine gun
Armour:	16mm–152mm
Sustained road speed:	13.5mph
Max. range on roads:	142 miles
Total built:	not known

Chapter 15

M4A1(75) Sherman Tank
Bayeux

Location: Bayeux 14400, Boulevard Fabien Ware.

This tank is on display at the Battle of Normandy Memorial Museum (le Musée Mémorial de la Bataille de Normandie) near the large Bayeux War Cemetery. The M4A1 Sherman Tank was powered by a petrol Continental R975 C1 9-cylinder radial engine that produced 400hp. It had a top road speed of 30mph (48km/h). It had an operational range of around 120 miles (193km). The tank had a crew of five: commander, driver, gunner, loader and co-driver/machine gunner. Its armour thickness ranged from 12.7mm to 76.2mm. It was armed with the standard 75mm M3 gun and two .30cal Browning M1919A4 machine guns, one in the hull and the other next to the main gun in the turret.

What is unusual about this M4A1 Sherman tank is that it has 'duckbill' extensions fitted to the track. These widened the track to increase the surface area and help the tank cross waterlogged, muddy or snow-covered fields and tracks. It helped stop the tank sinking down into the soft ground by spreading out the load. German tanks also used track extensions. The coaxial and hull machine guns fitted to this tank are replica weapons. Notice that it has an additional rectangular plate of armour welded onto both sides of the tank. This was to help increase the armour protection for the driver and co-driver positions.

The Sherman was designed to be easy to maintain. The final drives and transmission at the front of the tank could be accessed by unbolting the front lower hull curved armour plate and a new one fitted. If the road wheels or suspension system were damaged by an anti-tank mine, the crew just unscrewed 16 securing bolts and swapped out the bogie. Unlike the Germans, who could transport damaged tanks by railroad back to the factory that built them to be overhauled, U.S. tanks needed to be relatively reliable. All tanks break down, but U.S.-built tanks need to be fixed in the field. This is why many parts used in the construction of the Sherman tank were not new. The engineers just improved the design of parts they knew already worked on earlier vehicles.

There is a plaque by the tank that says, 'M4A1 Sherman Tank given to honour the sacrifices of the past that have provided hope for the future. Presented by H.Q. VII Corps U.S. Army'.

Specifications	
Length:	5.84m
Width:	2.31m
Height:	2.74m
Weight:	29.8 tons
Engine:	Continental R975 CI, 9-cylinder, 4-cycle, radial 400hp petrol engine
Crew:	5
Main gun:	75mm gun M3 in an M34 mount
Other weapons:	Two .30cal MG M1919A4 machine guns; one .50cal MG HB M2 machine gun
Armour:	12.7mm–76.2mm
Sustained road speed:	21mph
Max. range on roads:	120 miles
Total built:	6,281

Chapter 16

3 inch Gun Motor Carriage M10
Bayeux

Location: Bayeux 14400, Boulevard Fabien Ware.

This 3 inch Gun Motor Carriage M10 tank destroyer is on display at the Battle of Normandy Memorial Museum (le Musée Mémorial de la Bataille de Normandie) near the large Bayeux War Cemetery. After the war, this M10 was shipped back to England, where it was purchased by Pounds Shipowners and Shipbreakers Ltd of Portsmouth for scrap metal. It was rescued from their Portsmouth scrapyard, restored and mounted on a concrete plinth that is surrounded by a low hedge. The engine covers at the rear of the M10 are not original. A large metal plate has been welded over the engine compartment. The hull identification number '1662' is stamped into the rear towing eyes. The fictitious number 'USA 12345678' is painted on the side. It previously had the number 'USA 40623102'. Painted on the front of this M10 is 'V602TD' and 'D-9'.

The 3in (76.2mm) M7 Gun on the M10 needed a counterweight at the rear of the turret. It was powered by a General Motors 6046 diesel (conjoined twin 6-71s) engine that produced 375hp. This gave the M10 a top road speed of 32mph (51km/h). It had an operational road range of 200 miles (321km) and a crew of five: commander, driver and three gunners. It was produced between 1942 and 1943 and 4,993 M10s and 1,713 M10A1s were made. It was used right up to the end of the war.

These open-topped M10s were not designed to be at the front of an attack. They would cover the flank of an attack in case of a counter-attack from defensive positions that enabled them to use a 'shoot and scoot' tactic. They had better speed than a tank but thinner armour. Each U.S. tank destroyer battalion had 36 vehicles divided into three companies, as well as a reconnaissance company of jeeps and armoured scout cars to help ferret out the disposition of enemy armour so that the battalions could move into position. The Allied forces officially used the designation '3in Gun Motor Carriage M10'. The name 'Wolverine' is a post-war name for the M10; it has not been found on any wartime document.

Specifications	
Length:	6.82m
Width:	3.04m
Height:	2.89m
Weight:	29.1 tons
Engine:	GM Series 71, Model 6046, twin in-line 375hp diesel engine
Crew:	5
Main gun:	76.2mm gun M7 in M5 Mount
Other weapons:	One .50cal (12.7mm) MG HB M2 Browning machine gun and provision for five .30cal Carbine M1 rifles
Armour:	9.5mm–57.2mm
Sustained road speed:	25mph
Max. range on roads:	200 miles
Total built:	4,993 M10s and 1,713 M10A1

Chapter 17

25pdr Sexton Self-Propelled Artillery Gun
Bayeux

Location: Bayeux 14400, Boulevard Fabien Ware.

This 25pdr Sexton self-propelled gun (SPG) is on display at the Battle of Normandy Memorial Museum (le Musée Mémorial de la Bataille de Normandie) near the large Bayeux War Cemetery. The Canadian 25pdr Sexton gradually replaced the American-built 105mm M7 Priest self-propelled artillery gun used by the British, Polish and Commonwealth forces. Having to rely upon American supplies of 105mm shells could be problematic. To ease the logistics chain, the Sexton was chosen as the standard self-propelled artillery gun, as the towed guns in use by the Royal Artillery units were Quick-Firing (QF) 25pdrs. Sextons were used in Italy as well as during the invasion of Normandy on 6 June 1944.

Painted on the hull side is the registration number S-233841, but on the front of the superstructure is the name 'Raclawice' and 'Serial 38050'. It is painted in Polish Army markings. The museum obtained this Sexton 25pdr self-propelled artillery gun from Pounds Shipowners and Shipbreakers Ltd scrapyard in Portsmouth, England.

The first Sexton SPG was based on the American M3 Lee tank, but later versions used the hull of the Canadian-built Sherman Grizzly tank. It was powered by a Continental R975 9-cylinder radial petrol engine that produced 400hp. It had a top speed of 25 mph (40km/h) and had a crew of six: commander, driver, gunner, gun-layer, loader and radio operator. They were protected from small arms fire, high explosive and mortar shell shrapnel by armour that ranged in thickness from 12.7mm to 50.8mm. The top of the vehicle was open, but the crew could cover the top with a tarpaulin in bad weather.

The Sexton hull was identical to the that of the Ram in early production vehicles, with a welded superstructure. Changes introduced during production included the adoption of a one-piece cast nose (as on late M4 medium tanks), M4 type bogies with trailing return rollers, a towing hook at the rear for ammunition trailers, provision of an auxiliary generator, stowage for extra equipment, and mounts for Bren AA machine guns. Sextons remained in British and Canadian service for many years post-war.

Specifications	
Length:	6.12m
Width:	2.71m
Height:	2.43m
Weight:	25.44 tons
Engine:	Continental R975 C4 9-cylinder, 4-cycle, radial 400hp petrol engine
Crew:	6
Main gun:	Royal Ordnance QF 25pdr Mk.II or Mk.III
Other weapons:	.303in Bren light machine gun
Armour:	12.7mm–50.8mm
Sustained road speed:	21mph
Max. range on roads:	125 miles
Total built:	Approximately 2,000

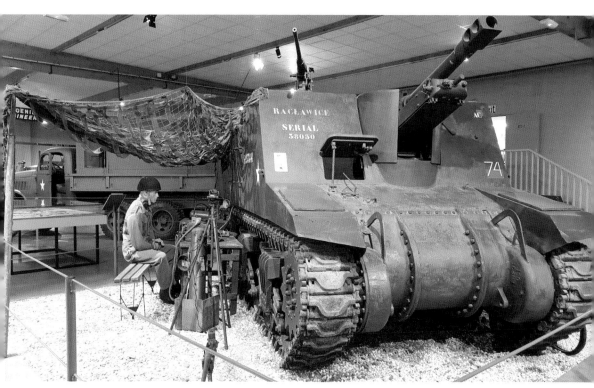

Chapter 18

Jagdpanzer 38 Hetzer G13 Tank Destroyer
Bayeux

Location: Bayeux 14400, Boulevard Fabien Ware.

This tank destroyer is on display at the Battle of Normandy Memorial Museum (le Musée Mémorial de la Bataille de Normandie) near the large Bayeux War Cemetery. The German Jagdpanzer 38 tank destroyer did not take part in the defence of Normandy. It first entered service on the Eastern Front in July 1944. It is strange that the Bayeux Memorial Museum of the Battle of Normandy decided to place one outside the museum.

This is not a wartime Jagdpanzer 38 tank destroyer. If you look at the front two curved cast final drive casings behind the track final drive sprocket, you will see a maintenance hole covered with a bolt. This identifies this vehicle as being a Swiss Army contract G13 Hetzer that was built in Czechoslovakia (now the Czech Republic) after World War Two. The G13 muzzle brake has been removed to make it look more like the World War Two Jagdpanzer 38 tank destroyer configuration. If you look at the end of the gun barrel, you can still see the screw thread. It was armed with a high-velocity, powerful and accurate 7.5cm Panzerjägerkanone 39 L/48 (7.5cm Pak 39 L/48) anti-tank.

In 1946 the Swiss Army placed an order with the new Czechoslovakian government for 158 Jagdpanzer 38 tank destroyers. They would become known as the G-13 Hetzer. A few were built using wartime Jagdpanzer 38 tank destroyer hulls that had been constructed before the war ended. Most of the contract used new hulls. Ninety-four of them were re-engined with diesel power packs. In 1970, when the G13 Hetzers finished operational service with the Swiss Army, they were offered for sale. Military collectors and museums purchased them and passed them off as World War Two German Hetzer Jagdpanzers just like the one at the Bayeux Memorial Museum of the Battle of Normandy. During World War Two, the term 'Hetzer' was not an official term used in the majority of German documents. The name became popular after the war. 'Hetzer' is a German country sport hunting term that means a fast chaser of prey. The Jagdpanzer 38 was a slow ambush weapon. The nickname was wrongly applied to this vehicle as it did not relate to its role.

Specifications	
Length:	6.27m
Width:	2.63m
Height:	2.10m
Weight:	17.63 tons
Engine:	Praga EPA AC 2800 6-cylinder 158hp petrol engine
Crew:	4
Main gun:	7.5cm Pak 39 L/48
Other weapons:	7.92mm MG34 machine gun
Armour:	8mm–60mm
Sustained road speed:	24.8mph
Max. range on roads:	111.8 miles
Total built:	2,827

Chapter 19

Wespe SPG, Flakpanzer 38(t) and Caterpillar D7
Bayeux

Location: Bayeux 14400, Boulevard Fabien Ware.

These vehicles are on display at the Battle of Normandy Memorial Museum (le Musée Mémorial de la Bataille de Normandie) near the large Bayeux War Cemetery. The museum's German 105mm Wespe artillery self-propelled gun and Flakpanzer 38(t) are displayed as wrecks.

The Wespe was a German Army artillery 10.5cm self-propelled gun based on the Panzer II light tank (Sd.Kfz.121) hull. Its full designation was 10.5cm Leichte Feldhaubitze 18/2 auf Fahrgestell Panzerkampfwagen II Selbstfahrlafette (Sd.Kfz.124), which was abbreviated to 10.5cm LeFH 18/2 auf Fgst. Pz.Kpfw II (Sf). It was given the nickname 'Wespe': German for wasp. They were built using obsolete Panzer II tank hulls.

The German Army needed artillery support. Horse-drawn artillery guns and towed artillery guns often got stuck in the mud or snow. Tracked self-propelled artillery guns could cross this testing terrain and keep up with the troops and tanks. They were also quicker to get ready for action. To tow one artillery gun required a team of six horses, three men to look after the horses and a gun crew of five or six men. A self-propelled gun mounted on a tracked hull only required the gun crew and some petrol. The army wanted self-propelled artillery guns. German industry came up with a number of different solutions, one of which was the Wespe.

The Flakpanzer 38(t) wreck belonged to the 12th SS Panzer Division. It was destroyed on 20 or 21 August 1944 near St-Lambert-sur-Dives. It was retrieved from the Trun scrapyard and renovated by the museum's team. The gun and the damaged front drive sprocket are probably not the original ones mounted on the vehicle. It was in a very poor rusted condition when discovered.

The Caterpillar D7 was first manufactured in America by Caterpillar Inc. in 1938. It was most commonly used as a bulldozer. The U.S. Army used armoured D7 bulldozers for earth moving, road building and clearing, airfield runway construction and beach obstacle removal. Between 1942 and 1945, 20,503 D7 Caterpillar dozers had been built.

Wespe SPG Specifications	
Length:	4.81m
Width:	2.28m
Height:	2.3m
Weight:	10.82 tons
Engine:	Maybach HL62 TR 6-cylinder 138hp petrol engine
Crew:	5
Main gun:	10.5cm LeFH 18/2 auf Fgst. Pz.Kpfw II (Sf) light field howitzer
Other weapons:	None
Armour:	5mm–30mm
Sustained road speed:	25mph
Max. range on roads:	137 miles
Total built:	676

Chapter 20

French APX Tank Turret Used in the German Atlantic Wall
Bayeux

Location: Bayeux 14400, Boulevard Fabien Ware.

This tank turret is on display at the Battle of Normandy Memorial Museum (le Musée Mémorial de la Bataille de Normandie) near the large Bayeux War Cemetery. It is part of an exhibition about the German fortifications along the Normandy coast known as the 'Atlantic Wall'. Many large-scale and smaller defensive structures used turrets from captured tanks as part of the design. The Atlantic Wall was not an unbroken barrier but rather a line of defences built by the German civilian and military engineering organisation called the 'TODT' after its founder Fritz Todt. It stretched from the top of Norway to the border with Spain. Work began in 1942 and was not completed when the Allies invaded Normandy on 6 June 1944.

The smaller bunkers, made from reinforced concrete, were known as a 'Tobruk'. They were designed to accommodate and shelter only a few soldiers. There was an observation opening at the top which was often covered by a tank turret. Although the turrets had guns, they were mainly used as a safe, armoured-protected observation post that enabled the soldier to scan the area he was supposed to be defending. Many were fitted with radios so he could report back enemy aircraft raids moving inland.

The standard APX turret (and variations of it) was used on the Hotchkiss H35 and H39, the Renault R35 and R40. All of these turrets were operated by one man. Access was gained through a large rear hatch rather than the normal arrangement of a hatch in the top of the turret as found on most other tanks of World War Two. The most common French tank main gun in 1940 was the 3.7cm Puteaux SA18 gun that was the same calibre as the gun mounted in the World War One Renault FT light tank's turret. However, this gun was now mounted in a new cast turret with thicker armour and cast mantlet. There were two versions of the Renault FT tank. One was armed with a machine gun and the other armed with a 3.7cm tank gun. They went into combat together so the gun tank could deal with fortified strongpoints and field gun batteries, while the machine-gun-armed tank could take on infantry and machine-gun nests. Tanks fitted with the APX turret could deal with all these threats as it was also fitted with a coaxial 7.5mm machine gun.

Early French tank turrets were constructed by riveting armoured plates to an internal metal frame. Welding was a new technology and not widely used. The introduction of armour casting to make tank turrets was an innovation that was hoped would lower production time and costs of tank manufacture. Initially these turrets were 30mm thick, but the armour thickness was increased to 40mm to protect the tank commander from the German 3.7mm anti-tank gun. This turret was used as a Tobruk in the Cherbourg area.

Chapter 21

105mm Howitzer Motor Carriage M7 Priest
Port-en-Bessin

Location: Port-en-Bessin 14520, L'Épinette, Musée des épaves sous-marines du débarquement (on the D6 about one mile south of Port-en-Bessin just north of the Châteaux La Chenevière restaurant).

The original owner of the D-Day Underwater Wrecks Museum (Musée des épaves sous-marines du débarquement) recovered many drowned armoured fighting vehicles from the bottom of the English Channel, near the Normandy D-Day beaches. He placed them in this museum as a memorial. The vehicles have purposely not been restored. The corrosion caused by the saltwater has been treated and stopped. Seeing the vehicles left in this condition makes the visitor question why they are like this. Inside the museum buildings, the story is told of what happened and the lives lost trying to free Europe from an evil dictatorship.

The M7 Priest was powered by a Continental R975 C1 petrol engine which produced 400hp. It had a top road speed of 24mph (39km/h) but only 15mph (24km/h) off-road. Its armour thickness ranged from 12.7mm to 50.8mm. The M7 was not designed to be at the front line of a battlefield, battling tanks. Its armour was only thick enough to protect the crew from small-arms fire and shrapnel from exploding enemy rocket, mortar and artillery fire.

The M7 Priest's main gun was a 105mm howitzer that could fire high-explosive shells 7 miles (11.27km). The M7 was not designed to be on the front line of a battlefield, battling tanks. Its armour was only thick enough to protect the crew from small-arms fire and shrapnel from exploding enemy rocket, mortar and artillery fire.

It was called the 105mm Howitzer Motor Carriage M7 in the U.S. Army. It was used by the British Army under the lend-lease agreement in the North African desert, Sicily and Italian campaigns. The British officially called it the '105mm Self-Propelled Gun, Priest'. The previous British SPGs had been called the 'Bishop' and 'Deacon'. The M7 had a machine gun in an armoured tower that looked like a church pulpit. This is why the British gave it the nickname 'Priest'.

Specifications	
Length:	6.01m
Width:	2.87m
Height:	2.94m
Weight:	22.58 tons
Engine:	Continental R975 C1 radial 9-cylinder 400hp petrol engine
Crew:	7
Main gun:	105mm M2A1 howitzer
Other weapons:	0.50cal (12.7mm) MG HB M2 Browning machine gun
Armour:	12.7mm–50.8mm
Sustained road speed:	21mph
Max. range on roads:	120 miles
Total built:	3,489

Chapter 22

M4(75) Sherman Dozer Tank
Port-en-Bessin

Location: Port-en-Bessin 14520, L'Épinette, Musée des épaves sous-marines du débarquement (on the D6 about one mile south of Port-en-Bessin just north of the Châteaux La Chenevière restaurant).

M4 Sherman tanks were fitted with bulldozer blades to clear beach obstructions as part of the D-Day attack on the German-held Normandy coast. Some never made it to the beach as their tank landing craft got hit by a mine or shell and sank.

The U.S. Army in North Africa realised that they needed bulldozers to help make airfields, clear roads, fill in bomb craters, move destroyed vehicles and tanks off roads, and clear rubble.

The Army came up with the idea of fitting a dozer blade to the front of a tank. Sherman dozers were first used in Italy in April 1944 during the landings at Anzio. In total, 1,957 tank bulldozer blades were manufactured during World War Two. Sherman dozers were used during the Battle of Normandy and all the way to Berlin. When tanks and supply vehicles could not cross ditches and anti-tank trenches, Sherman dozers were called in to fill those holes. On the D-Day beaches, they made roads through the sand dunes so equipment, men and tanks could get off the beaches and into the countryside to take objectives. They were also used to construct ramps of earth over the top of anti-tank obstacles and sea walls.

Tanks that were being used during the first waves of the assault on the Normandy beaches were made waterproof. The attachment of a bulldozer blade at the front of the tank did not interfere with the normal running of a waterproof tank. Sherman dozer tanks were often the first tanks of the tank landing craft. They deployed their dozer blade to remove beach obstructions while still in the water. This enabled the following tanks to get onto the sand quickly.

Any obstruction that could not be breached was ramped over. Large quantities of earth and sand were built up against the obstruction. Further earth and sand were pushed up the ramp and over the edge to make a ramp on the other side. Sherman dozers were also used to attack machine-gun pillboxes. The bullets bounced off the dozer blade, and the sand pushed in front of the blade was used to block up the hole.

M4(75) Sherman Specifications	
Length:	5.89m
Width:	2.61m
Height:	2.74m
Weight:	29.86 tons
Engine:	Continental R975 CI, 9-cylinder, 4-cycle, radial 400hp
Crew:	5
Main gun:	75mm gun M3 in a M34A1 mount
Other weapons:	Two .30cal MG M1919A4 machine guns; one .50cal MG HB M2 machine gun; one 2in mortar M3 (smoke)
Armour:	12.7mm–88.9mm
Sustained road speed:	21mph
Max. range on roads:	120 miles
Total built:	6,748 (total fitted with dozer blade not know)

Chapter 23

M4A1(75) Sherman DD Large Hatch Tank
Port-en-Bessin

Location: Port-en-Bessin 14520, L'Épinette, Musée des épaves sous-marines du débarquement (on the D6 about one mile south of Port-en-Bessin just north of the Châteaux La Chenevière restaurant).

The original owner of this marine scrapyard was Jacques Lemonchois. He had obtained the salvage rights to 50 per cent of the Normandy invasion coast. He owned a large boat with a crane fitted on top that had a giant claw. Divers would search the seabed for wrecks and direct the crane to that location to grab it and bring it onto the boat.

The hull of this drowned Sherman M4A1(75) Duplex Drive swimming tank has large crew hatches. The turret came from a different drowned U.S. 741st Tank Battalion, M4A1 Sherman DD tank. Its tank hull could not be recovered as it was buried too deep in sand. The recovery crew could only lift the turret off the seabed.

The Sherman M4A1 tank required a crew of five: commander, driver, gunner, loader, co-driver/hull machine gunner. Its main gun was a 75mm M3 gun that fired high-explosive artillery shells as well as armour-piercing rounds. This gun could not penetrate the front armour of a German Panther or Tiger tank. The Sherman also had two .30cal Browning M1919A4 machine guns, one in a ball mount in the hull and another coaxial next to the main gun in the turret. It had a cast hull and turret. Armour thickness ranged from 12.7mm to 76.2mm, but unlike some of the British tank designs that used vertical armour plates, the Sherman's armour was sloped at the front, giving the tank added protection without the negative effects of extra weight.

The DD tank worked by erecting a canvas flotation screen around the tank using a system of compressed air bottles and pipes that inflated long rubber tubes to provide the screen with rigidity. It took around 15 minutes to inflate but could be collapsed very rapidly the moment the tank reached the shore. Two propellers were fitted to the rear of the tank hull and were powered by the tank's engine. American forces plus British and Commonwealth troops used Sherman tanks fitted with Duplex-Drives and flotation screens.

Specifications	
Length:	5.84m
Width:	2.31m
Height:	2.74m
Weight:	29.8 tons
Engine:	Continental R975 C1, 9-cylinder, 4-cycle, radial 400hp petrol engine
Crew:	5
Main gun:	75mm gun M3 in an M34 mount
Other weapons:	Two .30cal MG M1919A4 machine guns; one .50cal MG HB M2 machine gun
Armour:	12.7mm–76.2mm
Sustained road speed:	21mph
Max. range on roads:	120 miles
Total built:	6,281

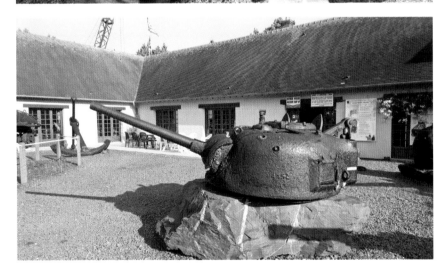

Chapter 24

Stuart M5A1 Tank
Port-en-Bessin

Location: Port-en-Bessin 14520, L'Épinette, Musée des épaves sous-marines du débarquement (on the D6 about one mile south of Port-en-Bessin just north of the Châteaux La Chenevière restaurant).

The most numerous light tank used by the Allies in the D-Day invasion of Normandy was the American-built Stuart tank that was sometimes called a 'Honey tank' by the British. This is an M5A1 Stuart light tank.

Jacques Lemonchois owned a marine scrapyard. He had purchased the salvage rights to 50 per cent of the sunken tanks, vehicles, guns and ships that had sunk to the bottom of the sea on the Normandy invasion coast. He owned a large boat with a crane fitted on top that had a giant claw. He was a diver and employed other divers to help him search the seabed for wrecks. When one was found half-submerged in the sandy bottom, they would direct the crane to that location to grab it and bring it onto the boat.

Many visitors to the museum question why the tanks have not been restored and are left out in the open. These tanks are displayed as a memorial to those crews who lost their lives at sea. Many tanks did not make it to the Normandy beaches. Ships and tank landing craft hit coastal defence mines or were shelled and sank. The corrosion caused by the saltwater has been treated and the bodywork protected from further decay. This is the only museum that tells this aspect of the D-Day landings story.

Stuart light tanks were used as scout tanks for reconnaissance work. They used their speed to get out of trouble and avoid becoming targets. This did not always work. Reconnaissance units would be sent ahead to see if bridges were still intact and prevent them from being blown up by attacking the enemy engineers and infantry by the bridge. They would advance until they made contact with German forces and then radio back for help or an artillery barrage.

The tank was armed with a 37mm M6 gun and three machine guns: one .30cal Browning M1919A4 in a ball mount in the hull, another .30cal Browning M1919A4 in a flexible AA mount on the roof and a .30cal Browning M1919A5 coaxial next to the 37mm gun in the turret.

Specifications	
Length:	4.83m
Width:	2.28m
Height:	2.56m
Weight:	15.5 tons
Engine:	Twin Cadillac Series 42, V8, air-cooled, 296hp petrol engine
Crew:	4
Main gun:	3.7cm M6 gun
Other weapons:	Two .30cal Browning M1919A4 machine guns; one .30cal Browning M1919A5 machine gun
Armour:	9.5mm–51mm
Sustained road speed:	36mph
Max. range on roads:	100 miles
Total built:	6,810

Chapter 25

Sherman M4(75) Rhino Tank
Catz

Location: Catz, Avenue du Cotentin junction with Rue de la Fourchette, Saint Hilaire Petitville 50500 Normandy Victory Museum.

The Normandy Victory Museum was built on a wartime USAAF A10 airfield. It has a number of exhibits on display outside, including a Sherman M4(75) tank fitted with a hedgerow cutter. The blade was known as the Rhinoceros, Rhino or Culin Cutter after U.S. Army Sergeant Curtis G. Culin of the 2nd Armored Division who is attributed with its design. This Sherman M4(75) has the serial number '1940' and was built by Baldwin Locomotive Works, Eddystone, Pennsylvania, USA, in February 1943. They were also fitted to M3 Stuart light tanks and M10 tank destroyers.

Allied forces became bogged down in the Normandy bocage country: a landscape of small, irregularly sized, thick hedgerow-lined fields and sunken lanes. Most fields only had one entrance. The Germans would hide in the trees and hedgerow opposite it. As soon as an Allied soldier or tank entered the field, they would come under attack by machine-gun bullets, armour-piercing rounds or high-explosive shellfire. The Rhino blade enabled attacking troops to smash through the boundary hedges at an unexpected spot and take the waiting enemy by surprise. They were initially fabricated in Normandy but were later manufactured in Britain and attached to tanks heading to Europe. This tank is on loan from the Musée des Blindés (The Armour Museum), Saumur, France.

The initial assault on the D-Day beaches was by infantry transported in landing craft. The Normandy Victory Museum has a late-production example on display on the old airfield. It is a Landing Craft, Vehicle Personnel (LCVP) Higgins Boat. Nearly 24,000 LCVPs were produced by Higgins Industries in New Orleans, Louisiana, USA. They measured 11m in length. They were armed with two .30cal Browning machine guns and operated by two crewmen. It could carry either 36 infantrymen, a jeep and 12 men or up to 3.57 tons of cargo.

Also on display is a U.S. Army engineer's Caterpillar D7 tracked bulldozer. They were used for many different tasks, ranging from clearing beach obstacles and making roads to constructing airfields. This is an unarmoured version. It would be used behind the front line. In combat situations, tanks were fitted with dozer blades to clear obstacles.

Specifications	
Length:	5.89m
Width:	2.61m
Height:	2.74m
Weight:	29.86 tons
Engine:	Continental R975 CI, 9-cylinder, 4-cycle, radial 400hp
Crew:	5
Main gun:	75mm gun M3 in an M34A1 mount
Other weapons:	Two .30cal MG M1919A4 machine guns; one .50cal MG HB M2 machine gun; one 2in mortar M3 (smoke)
Armour:	12.7mm–88.9mm
Sustained road speed:	21mph
Max. range on roads:	120 miles
Total built:	6,748

(Photographs © Albert Pujadas)

Chapter 26

M4A1(76) VVSS Sherman
Overlord Museum, Colleville-sur-Mer

Location: Colleville-sur-Mer 14710, Route d'Omaha Beach junction with Route du Cimetiere Americain.

This restored M4A1(76) Vertical Volute Spring System (VVSS) Sherman tank was fitted with the longer, more powerful high-velocity 76mm gun rather than the standard, shorter barrelled 75mm gun that was mounted in the vast majority of Sherman tanks. Although they had been shipped directly to England from the American factories that built them in early 1944, they were not used on D-Day. The U.S. armoured divisions had spent most of their time familiarising themselves and training on Sherman tanks armed with the 75mm gun. It was felt that issuing a new type of Sherman tank would cause training and logistical problems as the new tank variant needed to be supplied with different ammunition.

After initial tank-on-tank combat reports were analysed by the U.S. Army High Command in Europe, it was quickly realised they needed a tank with a better gun. General Bradley ordered that the M4A1(76) VVSS Sherman tanks being stored in England were to be shipped to Normandy. They first saw combat in Operation *Cobra*, the American breakout from the beachheads, seven weeks after the D-Day landings.

To increase firepower, the U.S. Army Ordnance Department developed the 76mm gun M1 and the M1A1, starting in July 1942. Tests showed that the existing M4 series turret was too small to accommodate the extra length of this weapon, and the turret of the T20/T23 medium tank was adopted and suitably modified. The 76mm gun installation was standardised and introduced in production lines from early 1944. The suffix '(76)' was introduced to indicate tanks armed with this gun. The flash, smoke and dust stirred up when the gun was fired, caused a few problems. The gunner found it hard to track a shot and make corrections because he could not see where it landed. This problem was solved by adding a muzzle brake that deflected some of the explosive flame and gases sideways. A modified 76mm gun M1A1C or M1A2 with a muzzle brake was introduced later in the war.

The M4A1 Sherman Tank armour thickness ranged from 12.7mm to 88.9mm. It was powered by a petrol Continental R975 C4 9-cylinder radial engine that produced 400hp.

Specifications	
Length:	7.46m
Width:	2.66m
Height:	2.97m
Weight:	31.51 tons
Engine:	Continental R975 C4, 9-cylinder, 4-cycle, radial 400hp petrol engine
Crew:	5
Main gun:	76mm gun M1A1, M1A1C or M1A2 in an M62 mount
Other weapons:	Two .30cal MG M1919A4 machine guns; one .50cal MG HB M2 machine gun; one 2in Mortar M3 (smoke)
Armour:	12.7mm–88.9mm
Sustained road speed:	21mph
Max. range on roads:	100 miles
Total built:	3,426

Chapter 27

3 inch Gun Motor Carriage M10
Overlord Museum, Colleville-sur-Mer

Location: Colleville-sur-Mer 14710, Route d'Omaha Beach junction with Route du Cimetiere Americain.

The Overlord Museum and the Falaise Museum were set up by members of the Leloup family. The Leloup collection was started by the late Michel Leloup. Involved in logging timber after World War Two, he had access to scrapped and abandoned German Army vehicles and engines. Thankfully, Michel decided to collect one or two and start his own private collection before they were all turned into scrap metal. The collection grew from there. They were housed and put on display at an old cheese factory in Falaise, Normandy, called Musée Aout 1944. His dream was to build a new museum near the Normandy beaches, as the Falaise building was not in a good location and was in need of expensive repair. His son, Nicolas Leloup, took over the collection when Michel died just as the family were in the early stages of securing a new museum site at Colleville.

This 3 inch Gun Motor Carriage M10 tank destroyer was armed with a 3in (76.2mm) M7 gun that could fire high-explosive shells as well as armour-piercing rounds. It could provide artillery support as well as act as a mobile tracked anti-tank gun. The longer gun on the M10 tank destroyer needed a counterweight at the rear of the turret. The crew were provided with a .50cal (12.7mm) Browning MG HB M2 machine gun that affixed to the top of the turret.

These open-topped M10s were not designed to be at the front of an attack. They would cover the flank of an attack in case of a counter-attack from defensive positions that enabled them to use a 'shoot and scoot' tactic. They had better speed than a tank but thinner armour. Each U.S. tank destroyer battalion had 36 vehicles divided into three companies, as well as a reconnaissance company of jeeps and armoured scout cars to help ferret out the disposition of enemy armour so that the battalions could move into position. The Allied forces officially used the designation, '3 inch Gun Motor Carriage M10'. The name 'Wolverine' is mainly a post-war name for the M10. That name has not been found on any wartime document.

Specifications	
Length:	6.82m
Width:	3.04m
Height:	2.89m
Weight:	29.1 tons
Engine:	GM Series 71, Model 6046, twin in-line 375hp diesel engine
Crew:	5
Main gun:	76.2mm gun M7 in M5 mount
Other weapons:	One .50cal (12.7mm) MG HB M2 Browning machine gun and provision for five .30cal Carbine M1 rifles
Armour:	9.52mm–57.15mm
Sustained road speed:	25mph
Max. range on roads:	200 miles
Total built:	6,706

Chapter 28

Sexton Self-Propelled Artillery Gun
Overlord Museum, Colleville-sur-Mer

Location: Colleville-sur-Mer 14710, Route d'Omaha Beach junction with Route du Cimetiere Americain.

This 25pdr Sexton artillery self-propelled gun was rescued from being cut up into scrap metal by the late Michel Leloup. While working in the forestry business after World War Two, he would come across many armoured vehicles, both German and Allied, that had been left on the battlefields of Normandy. Thankfully Michel decided to recover a few and start his own private collection. They were initially housed and put on display at an old cheese factory called Musée Aout 1944 in Falaise, Normandy. His dream was to build a new museum near the Normandy beaches as the Falaise building was not in a good location and was in need of expensive repair. His son, Nicolas Leloup, took over the collection when Michel died just as the family were in the early stages of securing a new museum site at Colleville. It was a shame Michel did not live long enough to see his dream come to life.

This Sexton was restored and painted with Canadian artillery tactical markings. The blue and red square with the number 76 is slightly wrong. The blue should be at the bottom and the red at the top. This would be the sign for the Regimental Headquarters. The number 76 indicated that the Sexton belongs to the Canadian 4th Armoured Division, 23rd Field Regiment (Self-Propelled). The square above is correct and indicated this Sexton belonged to the 1st battery, and the letter C shows that it was part of the 1st troop.

The first Sexton SPG was based on the American M3 Lee tank, but then the Canadian-built M4 Sherman Grizzly tank. It was powered by a Continental R975 C4 9-cylinder, 4-cycle, radial petrol engine that produced 400hp. It had a top speed of 25mph (40km/h). It had a crew of six: commander, driver, gunner, gun-layer, loader and radio operator. They were protected from small-arms fire, high-explosive and mortar shell shrapnel by armour that ranged in thickness from 12.7mm to 50.8mm.

The gun was an Ordnance QF 25pdr (87.6mm) Mk.II. The Sexton carried 105 rounds, mainly high-explosive shells. Some were smoke rounds, and a few were armour-piercing rounds.

Specifications	
Length:	6.12m
Width:	2.71m
Height:	2.43m
Weight:	25.44 tons
Engine:	Continental R975 C4 9-cylinder, 4-cycle, radial 400hp petrol engine
Crew:	6
Main gun:	Royal Ordnance QF 25pdr Mk.II or Mk.III
Other weapons:	.303inch Bren light machine gun
Armour:	12.7mm–50.8mm
Sustained road speed:	21mph
Max. range on roads:	125 miles
Total built:	Approx. 2,000

Chapter 29

Panther Ausf.A
Overlord Museum, Colleville-sur-Mer

Location: Colleville-sur-Mer 14710, Route d'Omaha Beach junction with Route du Cimetiere Americain.

This Panzer V Panther tank Ausf.A, hull number 152451, was built by Daimler-Benz between April and May 1944. It is believed that this Panther was originally one of the 12 Panther tanks given to the Musée des Blindés (The Armour Museum) in Saumur. In 1988 the damaged hull was exchanged for a Hanomag Sonderkraftfahrzeug Sd.kfz 251 German half-track that belonged to the Musée Aout 1944 military museum in Falaise, Normandy. Luckily the Panther was not left sitting outside rusting away. It was moved to an inside storage area. When the museum closed in 2012 it was transported to the new Overlord Museum who partially restored the tank and placed it in a diorama representing a field repair unit of the Wehrmacht, along with an original German field gantry crane.

It arrived in January 2013 and work started to remove the rust and repaint the vehicle. The 75mm tank gun barrel came from the Perpignan area of southern France. The Panther's turret is not the same one that was fitted to the hull when it was built in 1944. The original turret from this hull was used to restore the Musée des Blindés (The Armour Museum) Panther Tank number 254. This Panther served in the French Army after the war, until about 1955.

The hull used for the early production Panzer V Ausf.A was precisely the same as that used for the earlier Ausf.D. This new batch of Panther tanks were given the designation 'Ausf.A' because they were fitted with an improved turret.

Many features of the Ausf.D, such as the drum-shaped commander's cupola and the thin rectangular 'letterbox' hull machine gun port were still present on early production Ausf.A Panthers produced between July and December 1943. They only changed mid-production and not at the same time. Other modifications were introduced during the production run. Ausf.D and Ausf.A Panther tanks were also upgraded with different features once they had been issued to a Panzer division.

In late November 1943, a ball-mounted machine gun with a spherical armoured guard replaced the 'letterbox' opening on the factory production line. Next to the Panther is a Panzer IV Ausf.H turret with a 75mm L/48 gun.

Specifications	
Length:	8.86m
Width:	3.42m
Height:	3.10m
Weight:	50 tons
Engine:	Maybach HL 230 V12 700hp petrol engine
Crew:	5
Main Gun:	7.5cm Kw.K.42 L/70
Other weapons:	Two 7.92mm MG34 machine guns
Armour:	16mm–80mm (Turret front 100mm–110mm)
Sustained road speed:	34mph
Max. range on roads:	124 miles
Total built:	2,200

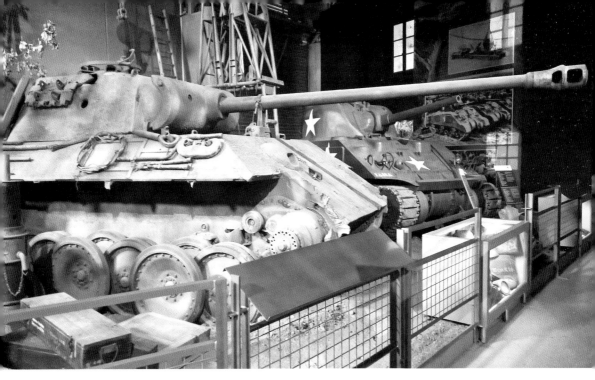

Chapter 30

Panzer IV Ausf.H
Overlord Museum, Colleville-sur-Mer

Location: Colleville-sur-Mer 14710, Route d'Omaha Beach junction with Route du Cimetiere Americain.

This German Panzer IV Ausf.H tank was rescued from being cut up into scrap metal by the Musée des Blindés (The Armour Museum) in Saumur. The tank was put on display inside the Musée Aout 1944 war museum in Falaise. When the museum closed in 2012 it was restored and transported to the new Overlord Museum close to Omaha Beach near the small village of Colleville-sur-Mer, Normandy. It arrived at its new home in March 2013.

The Panzer IV was the most common tank used against the Allies in the battle for Normandy in summer 1944. The Ausf.H was equipped with the high-velocity long-barrelled Kw.K.40 L/48 gun that could fire high-explosive shells as well as armour-piercing rounds. It was built with two 7.92mm MG34 machine guns, one next to the main gun in the turret and another in a ball mounting in the hull. The tank was subsequently registered as the Sd.Kfz. 161/2 by the German ordnance department.

The Panzer IV Ausf.H was powered by a 12-cylinder Maybach HL 120 TRM V12 engine that produced 256hp. It had an operational range of around 124 miles (210km). The tank had a crew of five: commander, driver, gunner, loader, hull machine-gunner/radio operator. They were protected by armour that ranged in thickness from 8mm to 80mm. It weighed 25 tonnes. By the end of 1943, anti-magnetic mine Zimmerit paste was factory-applied, new pre-air filters were fitted, along with a turret anti-aircraft mount for an extra MG34 (*Fliegerbeschussgerat*). The Panzer IV tank was produced in various different versions from 1936 to 1945. Over 2,414 were built.

If you have a look at the turret, you will see that additional spaced armour was added around the outside of the turret. The tank would also have had large panels of 5mm-thick *Schürzen* skirt armour plates that covered the hull and tracks. These have not been fitted on this restored Panzer IV example. They were designed to protect the tank from Soviet anti-tank rifles on the Eastern Front. The additional armour plating would take out the energy in the anti-tank round so that it could no longer penetrate the tank hull or turret.

Specifications	
Length:	7.02m
Width:	2.88m
Height:	2.68m
Weight:	25 tons
Engine:	Maybach HL 120 TRM V12 265hp petrol engine
Crew:	5
Main Gun:	7.5cm Kw.K.40 L/48
Other weapons:	Two 7.92mm MG34 machine guns
Armour:	8mm–80mm (80mm hull front)
Sustained road speed:	15.5mph (max. road speed: 24mph)
Max. range on roads:	124 miles
Total built:	2,414 approx.

Chapter 31

M4A1(76) VVSS Sherman Tank
Overlord Museum, Colleville-sur-Mer

Location: Colleville-sur-Mer 14710, Route d'Omaha Beach junction with Route du Cimetiere Americain.

This M4A1(76) VVSS Sherman tank has a post-war French Army serial number stamped on its hull and looks like it served with them for a period of time during the Cold War before being replaced by more modern tanks. It was rescued from being destroyed on a French Army firing range and then cut up into scrap metal by the late Michel Leloup. He displayed it outside the entrance to the Musée Aout 1944 – an old cheese factory in Falaise, Normandy. After his death, his son, Nicolas Leloup, took over the collection and transported this tank to the new Overlord Museum site at Colleville-sur-Mer.

This Sherman tank was fitted with the longer, more powerful high-velocity 76mm gun rather than the standard, shorter-barrelled 75mm gun that was mounted in the vast majority of Sherman tanks. Although they had arrived in England in early 1944, they were not used on D-Day. The U.S. armoured divisions had spent most of their time familiarising themselves and training on Sherman tanks armed with the 75mm gun. It was felt that issuing a new type of Sherman tank would cause training and logistical problems, as the new tank variant needed to be supplied with different ammunition.

After initial tank-on-tank combat reports were analysed by the U.S. Army High Command in Europe, it was quickly realised they needed a tank with a better gun. General Bradley ordered that the M4A1(76) VVSS Sherman tanks being stored in England were to be shipped over to Normandy. They first saw combat in Operation *Cobra*, the American breakout from the beachheads, seven weeks after the D-Day landings. The 2nd and 3rd U.S. Armored Divisions received approximately 60 M4A1(76) VVSS Sherman tanks each, which would be evenly distributed among their tank units.

The M4A1 Sherman tank was fitted with a large cast metal turret to cope with the longer 76mm gun. The acronym 'VVSS' stands for vertical volute spring suspension. A volute spring is a compression spring in the form of a cone (a volute). Under compression the coils slide over each other, affording longer travel.

Specifications	
Length:	7.46m
Width:	2.66m
Height:	2.97m
Weight:	31.51 tons
Engine:	Continental R975 C4, 9-cylinder, 4-cycle, radial 400hp petrol engine
Crew:	5
Main gun:	76mm gun M1A1, M1A1C or M1A2 in an M62 mount
Other weapons:	Two .30cal MG M1919A4 machine guns; one .50cal MG HB M2 machine gun; one 2in mortar M3 (smoke)
Armour:	12.7mm–88.9mm
Sustained road speed:	21mph
Max. range on roads:	100 miles
Total built:	3,426

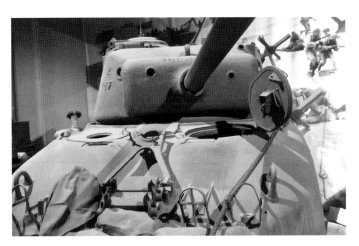

Chapter 32

M4A4T(75) Sherman Tank
Overlord Museum, Colleville-sur-Mer

Location: Colleville-sur-Mer 14710, Route d'Omaha Beach junction with Route du Cimetiere Americain.

This M4A4 Sherman tank was built by Chrysler in February 1943. Its hull number is 18723. It was armed with the standard 75mm M3 gun fixed into an M34 gun mount in the turret. (This was later changed to the M34A1 gun mount in later production tanks.) It could fire high-explosive artillery rounds as well as armour-piercing shells. It could penetrate the frontal armour of a Panzer IV tank but not the frontal armour on the Panther or Tiger tank; it could penetrate the side or rear armour of those tanks. This Sherman was also armed with two .30cal Browning M1919A machine guns. One was next to the main gun in the turret, whilst the other was in a ball mount in the hull.

The M4A4 Shermans were powered by a Chrysler A57 multibank 30-cylinder 4-cycle 'cloverleaf' water-cooled petrol engine. It was constructed using five car engines bolted together on a large metal frame. Its maximum net horsepower at 2,400rpm was 370hp, and it had a maximum gross horsepower rating at 2,850rpm of 425hp. The engine's maximum net torque was 1,020ft-lb at 1,200 propeller shaft rpm. Its maximum gross torque was 1,060ft-lb at 1,400 crankshaft rpm. It had a sustained road speed of 20mph and could go for short bursts up to 25mph. It had a fuel consumption of around 800 yards to the gallon or 2.2 gallons a mile.

The 1st and 5th French Armoured Divisions received M4A4s built in January/February 1943. This is believed to be one of those tanks. The designation of this tank was changed to M4A4T(75). The letter 'T' stands for the French word 'transformé'. By late spring of 1945, many of the power plants of the French Army's Sherman Tanks were wearing out. The only engine that was readily available from the U.S. was the Continental radial engine. The worn-out large Chrysler multibank engines were removed and the new replacement, smaller, Continental radial engines were fitted into position in the engine compartment. Internal modifications had to be made. These overhauled transformed tanks were called M4A4T(75) Transformé by the French Army and many were complete after the war.

Specifications	
Length:	6.05m
Width:	2.61m
Height:	2.74m
Weight:	31.11 tons
M4A4 Engine:	Chrysler A57 30-cylinder, 4-cycle, multibank 425hp petrol engine;
M4A4T(75) Engine:	Continental R975 radial engine
Crew:	5
Main gun:	75mm gun M3 in an M34 mount
Other weapons:	Two .30cal MG M1919A4 machine guns; one .50cal MG HB M2 machine gun
Armour:	12.7mm–76.2mm
Sustained road speed:	20mph
Max. range on roads:	100 miles
Total M4A4 built:	7,499 (Transformé conversions' total not known)

Chapter 33

M4A4T(75) Sherman Tank
Saint-Laurent-sur-Mer

Location: Saint-Laurent-sur-Mer 14710, Avenue de la Liberation (D517) junction with Chemin de Fossé Taillis. Musée Mémorial d'Omaha Beach.

This tank was given to the Musée Mémorial d'Omaha Beach by the Musée des Blindés (The Armour Museum) in Saumur. Its hull number is 18875. The tank's nickname, 'Burieux', can still be seen painted on the side. This tank was used by the French Army during and after the war. When its engine needed replacing, the original Chrysler A57 multibank 30-cylinder petrol engine was replaced with a Continental R975 radial engine. A letter 'T' was added to the tank's designation M4A4T(75). This stood for the French word 'transformé'.

Additional air filters were installed above the rear engine access doors. The original M4A4 engine deck plates were removed, and new plates added, which look like the plates found on M4s and M4A1 Sherman tanks. A hole was made in the rear hull plate, to be able to operate the starting handle for the radial engine (in order to remove the motor oil from the bottom of the engine cylinders). The rear mudguards were changed. The turret split hatch commander's cupola was replaced with a 'vision' cupola. The hull number found on the manufacturer's plate inside the tank was stamped on the front glacis plate. Three French 'factory plates' were welded to the front and back of the hull, and on the top of the turret. They record the factory and date of the upgrade. The letters 'A.B.S.' are an abbreviation for the factory Atelier de construction de Bourges, and 'A.R.L.' for the factory Atelier de construction de Rueil.

This M4A4 Sherman tank was built by Chrysler and armed with the standard 75mm M3 gun and was powered by a Chrysler A57 multibank 30-cylinder 4-cycle 'cloverleaf' water-cooled petrol engine. It was constructed using five car engines bolted together on a large metal frame. It had a sustained level road speed of 20mph and could go for short bursts up to 25mph. It had a fuel consumption of around 800 yards to the gallon or 2.2 gallons a mile. The M4A4 version of the Sherman tank was primarily used by the British and Commonwealth forces on D-Day.

Specifications	
Length:	6.05m
Width:	2.61m
Height:	2.74m
Weight:	31.11 tons
M4A4 Engine:	Chrysler A57 30-cylinder, 4-cycle, multibank 425hp petrol engine
M4A4T(75) Engine:	Continental R975 radial engine
Crew:	5
Main gun:	75mm gun M3 in an M34 mount
Other weapons:	Two .30cal MG M1919A4 machine guns; one .50cal MG HB M2 machine gun
Armour:	12.7mm–76.2mm
Sustained road speed:	20mph
Max. range on roads:	100 miles
Total M4A4 built:	7,499 ('Transformé conversions' total not known)

Chapter 34

Panther Turret Gun
Vierville-sur-Mer, D-Day Omaha Museum

Location: Vierville-sur-Mer 14710, Route de Grandchamp (D514) junction with La Hérode.

The Museum D-Day Omaha has a varied collection of large and small wartime artefacts. It was started by Michel Brissard, and his family took over after he died. Most of the items on display were abandoned and destined to be cut up for scrap metal. Michel took many years to build up his collection. Some exhibits that had been used on D-Day he discovered abandoned in other parts of France. A good example of this is the massive 'Whale' floating bridge. This was part of the Mulbury artificial port system. When transport ships docked by the side of the concrete harbour walls, the tanks and supply lorries would use the floating bridges to drive safely onto the beach. Five sections of these historic bridges, which could take the weight of a tank while floating in the sea, have been rescued.

In the outdoor section of the museum, you will discover Panther tank tracks and road wheels stacked up around a Panther gun barrel and mantlet. The Panther tank was armed with a long-barrelled high-velocity 7.5cm Kw.K.42 L/70 tank gun that could knock out most Allied and Soviet medium tanks at long distances. It had an effective direct fire range of 1.1km–1.3km. With a proficient, experienced crew, it could fire six rounds a minute. Seventy-nine rounds of 75mm ammunition could be stored inside the tank. The larger hole to the right of the main gun in the mantlet was for the coaxial 7.92mm MG34 machine gun. The gun was equipped with a muzzle brake at the end. The holes in the side enabled the explosive gases that built up behind a shell to be deflected sideways. This helped to reduce recoil and lengthened the service life of the gun barrel by reducing pressure.

The museum also has another famous German gun on display: the 88mm. Variations of this powerful weapon were fitted to the Tiger tank and Jagdpanther. The version on display is the towed 8.8cm flak anti-aircraft gun. It could fire high-explosive shells at enemy aircraft up to a maximum ceiling of 48,200ft. It was also an excellent long-range anti-tank gun.

The preserved bridge sections are not on display by the main museum building. You can see them lining the western side of the D517 road. Once you have finished looking around the museum, set your Sat Nav to Rue de la Percée, Vierville-sur-Mer. You will drive done the D517 and past the Mulbury Whale bridges on your left. Thousands of Allied troops, tanks, lorries, universal carriers, self-propelled guns and artillery guns went along those bridges in 1944. The Omaha Beach memorial is at the end of the road.

Opposite: Inside the Musée D-Day Omaha, a remote-controlled German Goliath tracked mine can be found. Its official designation is Leichter Ladungsträger Goliath. It was powered by a petrol/gasoline or electric engine. The operator directed it towards the target, and when it reached its destination, the 60kg or 100kg high-explosive payload would be detonated.

Chapter 35

M4A1(76) HVSS Sherman Tank
Utah Beach

Location: This is a difficult location to find using a navigation device. It is on the beach but not near a town. It is at the junction of a road called Utah Beach (D421) with the road Voie de la Liberté (D913). The museum is called Musée du Débarquement Utah Beach (Utah Beach Landing Museum), Plage de la Madeline, 50480 Sainte Marie du Mont.

This impressive-looking M4A1(76) Sherman tank did not land on Utah Beach on D-Day. It has not been confirmed that any arrived in mainland Europe before the war with Germany ended in May 1945. There are two photographs of two different M4A1(76) tanks in Europe, but the date they were taken is unknown. The M4A1(76) Sherman tank was fitted with the long-barreled high-velocity 76mm M1 gun. The tank had a .30cal Browning M1919A4 machine gun in a ball mount in the hull. What made this tank different from earlier Shermans was the width of the tracks. They were 23in (58.4cm) wide rather than the normal 16in (40.6cm). This helped decrease the tank's ground pressure and gave it a better ability to cross wet, muddy ground without sinking. They were also fitted with new Horizontal Volute Spring Suspension (HVSS).

On D-Day, sea conditions were rough. Sherman tanks fitted with the Duplex Drive (DD) and waterproof canvas skirts were not designed to swim through rough seas with high waves. Only two of the 32 DD Sherman tanks belonging to the U.S. 741st Tank Battalion reached Omaha Beach. Most of the others were swamped by waves coming over the top of the canvas skirt floating device.

Many men drowned, trapped in their tanks by the collapsing canvas and the weight of the water above them. Records show 27 of these DD tanks sank before they reached Omaha Beach. The two that landed on the beach were joined by three more that could not launch into the sea as the ramp on their LCT landing craft was damaged. The LCT took them straight onto the beach where they managed to get off the boat. The U.S. 743rd Tank Battalion was also issued with 32 DD Sherman tanks. Luckily, none of these tanks were launched into the sea after seeing the disaster that hit the U.S. 741st Tank Battalion DD tanks. They all landed directly onto the beach, under fire, at 6.40am. Nine of these tanks were knocked out in the fighting on D-Day. There were 23 left at the end of the day to carry on fighting.

Specifications	
Length:	7.46m
Width:	2.66m
Height:	2.97m
Weight:	31.51 tons
Engine:	Continental R975 C4, 9-cylinder, 4-cycle, radial 400hp petrol engine
Crew:	5
Main gun:	76mm M1A1, M1A1C or M1A2 gun in an M62 mount
Other weapons:	Two .30cal MG M1919A4 machine guns; one .50cal MG HB M2 machine gun; one 2in mortar M3 (smoke)
Armour:	12.7mm–88.9mm
Sustained road speed:	21mph
Max. range on roads:	100 miles
Total built:	3,426

Chapter 36

M4A2(75) Free French Sherman Tank
Utah Beach

Location: This is a difficult location to find using a navigation device. Try entering Saint-Martin-de-Varreville 50480, La Dune. It is next to the beach, just south-east of the junction of the D421 coast road and a road called La Dune (D423). It is called 'Monument du débarquement de la 2ème DB' (The Landing of the U.S. 2nd Armored Division Monument).

This memorial is to commemorate the Free French landings on Utah Beach and their battle casualties. The 2nd French Armoured Division (2e Division Blindée) did not land on D-Day but later, on 1 August 1944. The division was commanded by General Philippe Leclerc, and they joined General Pattons Third Army. The only Free French troops that landed on D-Day were the Green Berets' Kieffer Commando that took part in the liberation of Ouistreham,

The French 2e Division Blindée landed at Plage de le Saint-Martin-de-Varreville on the Utah Beach section of the Normandy coastline. The division comprised approximately 14,000 men, including 3,350 colonial troops, and was under the orders of General George S. Patton. It went on to be part of the liberation of Paris. The Allies allowed the 2e Division Blindée to be the first unit inside the capital following requests from General de Gaulle and Leclerc. On the night of 24 August 1944, the French forces advanced. There were many street fights on the way into the centre of the city. The French Resistance were attacking German soldiers in the capital. They arrived in the centre of the city at the Hotel de Ville just before midnight. U.S. forces followed. The Germans surrendered Paris on 25 August 1944.

The 2e Division Blindée fought battles in Lorraine, opened the Saverne Gap and liberated Strasbourg in eastern France. They then headed south and took part in the Colmar Pocket battles. The division was then transported across France to assist in the attack on the German-held French Atlantic port of Royan. They were then transported back to eastern France and took part in the final fighting in southern Germany and Austria in April 1945.

Specifications	
Length:	5.91m
Width:	2.61m
Height:	2.74m
Weight:	31.33 tons
Engine:	General Motors 6046 12-cylinder, 2-cycle, twin in-line, 410hp diesel engine
Crew:	5
Main gun:	75mm gun M3 in an M34A1 mount
Other weapons:	Two .30cal MG M1919A4 machine guns; one .50cal MG HB M2 machine gun; 2in mortar M3 (smoke)
Armour:	12.7mm–88.9mm
Sustained road speed:	25mph
Max. range on roads:	150 miles
Total built:	8,053

Chapter 37

M4A4(75) Sherman Tank
Sainte-Mère-Église

Location: Sainte-Mère-Église 50480, 14 Rue Eisenhower, Airborne Museum.

This M4A4 Sherman tank hull with M4A3(75)W high bustle turret replaced the M4A1(76) HVSS Sherman tank that had been on display at the World War Two D-Day landings display at the Airborne Museum Saint-Mère-Église. The museum wanted a Sherman tank armed with the standard 75mm gun as these types of tanks landed on the Normandy beaches in June 1944. Sherman tanks armed with the more powerful 76mm guns landed in Normandy seven weeks after the D-Day landings. The 2nd and 3rd U.S. Armored Divisions received approximately 60 M4A1(76) VVSS Sherman tanks each, which would be evenly distributed among their tank units. The M4A1(76) Sherman first saw combat in Operation *Cobra*, the American breakout from the beachheads.

Although the tank on display at the museum is not historically accurate, it does look more like the American Sherman tanks that were part of the U.S. armoured divisions that landed on Omaha and Utah beaches, and the ones that helped to reinforce the U.S. paratroopers who liberated the town of Sainte-Mère-Église at 4.30am on 6 June 1944. This French town was the first one to be liberated. Earlier that morning British paratroopers captured Ranville at 2.30am. It was the first French village to be liberated.

The town was tactically important as it lay on a major road junction for traffic going between Caen and Cherbourg. Sherman tanks that had landed on nearby Utah Beach with the U.S. VII Corps were soon passing through the newly liberated town on the way to the front. Some tanks stayed near the town to prevent it being retaken by a German counter-attack. 2nd Lieutenant Thomas J. Tighe of the 70th Tank Battalion received the Silver Star posthumously for his actions on the morning of 7 June 1944 while securing the town. He was killed when his tank was hit by German artillery fire.

The M4A4 Sherman had a longer hull than other Sherman tanks because it was powered by a Chrysler A57 multibank 30-cylinder 4-cycle 'cloverleaf' water-cooled petrol engine. It was constructed using five car engines bolted together on a large metal frame.

Specifications	
Length:	6.05m
Width:	2.61m
Height:	2.74m
Weight:	31.11 tons
Engine:	Chrysler A57 30-cylinder, 4-cycle, multibank 425hp petrol engine
Crew:	5
Main gun:	75mm gun M3 in an M34 mount
Other weapons:	Two .30cal MG M1919A4 machine guns; one .50cal MG HB M2 machine gun
Armour:	12.7mm–76.2mm
Sustained road speed:	20mph
Max. range on roads:	100 miles
Total built:	7,499

(Photographs © Amber Hopkins)

Chapter 38

Renault R35 Tank Replica
Sainte-Mère-Église

Location: Sainte-Mère-Église 50480, 14 Rue Eisenhower, Airborne Museum.

In the U.S. Airborne Museum in Sainte-Mère-Église, there is a fibreglass replica of a knocked-out French Renault R35 tank that had been used by the German Army and is used to tell the story of the La Fière bridge battle west of Sainte-Mère-Église.

The Germans launched a fierce counter-attack on D-Day against U.S. paratroopers holding Sainte-Mère-Église. Unfortunately, none of the three knocked-out, German-operated French tanks survived the hands of the post-war scrap-metal merchants. The Germans used the Renault R35 tank in a 'policing' role rather than a front line tank. In 1944 these tanks were considered obsolete, but to a lightly armed paratrooper, they were still a formidable threat.

On D-Day, in the early hours, A Company of the 505th Parachute Infantry Regiment, commanded by Lieutenant Dolan, along with some displaced men from the 507th and 508th regiments, attacked and captured the La Fière bridge. Later that day, German infantry and tanks returned to attack the bridge. An American 57mm gun, which had arrived by glider, had been set up on higher ground. It was spotted, and a high-explosive round from one of the tanks put it out of action.

Four U.S. paratroopers armed with two bazookas, positioned near the to the bridge, managed to knock out the advancing tanks. On 7 June 1944, following a sustained artillery bombardment, the Germans launched another counter-attack. The 505th Parachute Infantry Regiment suffered heavy losses but stood their ground. On 8 June 1944, the group of paratroopers defending the bridge received reinforcements from the 507th Parachute Infantry Regiment. The Germans continued to counter-attack.

On 9 June 1944, to secure control of the crossing, General Gavin launched an all-out assault over the flooded marshes. The casualties on both sides were horrific, but the men of the 507th Parachute Infantry Regiment and 325th Glider Infantry Regiment, supported by tanks brought in from Utah Beach, succeeded in occupying, once and for all, the village of Cauquigny on the other side. The battle at La Fière lasted for three days and has become legendary due to the ferocity of the combat and the huge losses incurred in men and equipment on both sides.

Specifications	
Length:	4.02m
Width:	1.87m
Height:	2.13m
Weight:	11.7 tons
Engine:	Renault 447 V4 85hp petrol engine
Crew:	2
Main gun:	3.7cm SA18 L/21 gun
Other weapons:	One 7.5mm MAC31 Reibel machine gun
Armour max.:	40mm
Sustained road speed:	12.4mph
Max. range on roads:	80 miles
Total built:	1,570

Chapter 39

Dead Man's Corner Museum
Saint-Côme-du-Mont

Location: Saint-Côme-du-Mont 50500, 2 Vierge de l'Amont (D913).

Sited on a hill, the museum overlooks the causeway that leads to the town of Carentan. In 1944 most of the fields were flooded marshland. The Germans decided to defend this location to stop an American breakout from the beachhead and prevent the forces on Utah and Omaha beaches joining up. A reconnaissance troop M5A1 Stuart tank went forward to scout out the location of the enemy at the junction. Unfortunately, the tank was knocked out by a German anti-tank gun at the junction of the Vierge de l'Amont road with Rue du Bel Esnault.

An internal explosion and fire killed the crew. The tank commander's body remained half hanging out of the commander's cupola on top of the turret. U.S. forces could not safely reach the tank until the German troops withdrew. The burned-out Stuart tank and the crew's corpses remained at the corner for several days before a graves registration team could remove, identify and designate a temporary cemetery for the burial of the four sets of remains. The horrible sight of the tank commander's charred body is why this location became known as 'Dead Man's Corner'.

The M5A1 Stuart tank is an amazing replica built by Patrick Letouzé. He used steel but, more surprisingly, concrete, for the tank's tracks. It is a static display 1:1 scale model but very realistic looking. It serves as a memorial for all those who lost their lives during the fighting in June 1944.

Next to the Dead Man's Corner Museum is the D-Day Experience Museum. Inside there is a fibreglass replica of an M4A1(75) Sherman tank built by Patrick Letouzé. Outside is a real Sherman tank. It is an M4A4T(75) Transformé used by the French Army after World War Two. Its original Chrysler multibank engine was removed and replaced with a smaller Continental radial engine.

The museum has restored to working condition, a Renault UE Chenillette armoured general-purpose tractor. It is painted as it would have looked on D-Day, in German camouflage and markings. The Germans could carry supplies and ammunition to the front line in the back of the vehicle or in a tracked towed trailer.

Specifications M5A1 Stuart	
Length:	4.62m
Width:	2.39m
Height:	2.33m
Weight:	17 tons
Engine:	Twin Cadillac V8 air-cooled 296hp petrol engine
Crew:	4
Main gun:	3.7cm M6 gun
Other weapons:	Three .30cal M1919 machine guns
Armour:	13mm–51mm
Sustained road speed:	36mph
Max. range on roads:	99 miles
Total built:	6,810

Chapter 40

M4A1(76) Sherman Tank
Camp Patton, Les Forges de Vardon

Location: This is a difficult place to find using a navigation device. Type in the name Les Forges de Vardon (in the prefecture of Manche, Normandy). It is the nearest settlement but is just a few houses on the crossroads of the D900 and D42. There is a big sign at this junction that points north up the D900: 'Camp Patton 1.5km'. As you drive up the D900, look for another, similar sign – 'Camp Patton 0.2km' – on the right, at the second set of crossroads you come to. It points down a small country lane. This is the D187 Rue de la Belle Manière. As you go down this lane, on the right around 200 yards, you will see the large M4A1(76) Sherman, by a sign that says 'Camp Patton'.

This M4A1(76) Sherman tank is part of a memorial to the soldiers under the command of General George S. Patton. He used this apple orchard clearing as his Third Army command post from 7 July to 2 August 1944, where he enjoyed complete secrecy and was able to plan, prepare and then command the Avranches Breakthrough and later Operation *Cobra*.

Patton secretly set up his headquarters here to help continue the deceit that he was still in England and was going to command the real invasion of France by landing troops at Calais. The German high command believed that Patton was the Allies' best commander. Wherever Patton was would be the location of the main invasion. The Allies had used Patton's high profile in the Press as a weapon of war to deceive the Germans as to the real location of the invasion. It worked. Hitler refused to release tanks and men on reserve near Calais to meet the invasion that had already occurred in Normandy until it was too late.

Patton lived in a truck trailer in the orchard along with his chief of staff, General Gaffey and General Gay, who all had their own trailers. Near these three trailers was a large tent used for meetings. Another tent was used for meals. Other officers and headquarters' staff were housed in tents pitched along the perimeter of the orchard. Latrines were dug. Military Police guarded the approaches to the orchard to stop any civilians getting close and discovering who was in command. The orchard was chosen as the trees hid the tents and buildings from German aircraft.

Specifications	
Length:	7.46m
Width:	2.66m
Height:	2.97m
Weight:	31.51 tons
Engine:	Continental R975 C4, 9-cylinder, 4-cycle, radial 400hp petrol engine
Crew:	5
Main gun:	76mm gun M1A1, M1A1C or M1A2 in an M62 mount
Other weapons:	Two .30cal MG M1919A4 machine guns; one .50cal MG HB M2 machine gun; one 2in mortar M3 (smoke)
Armour:	12.7mm–88.9mm
Sustained road speed:	21mph
Max. range on roads:	100 miles
Total built:	3,426

Chapter 41

M4A4T(75) Sherman Tank
Place Patton, Avranches

Location: Place Patton (Rue du General Patton Junction with Rue de la 4e Division Blindée Américaine).

This Sherman M4A4T(75) tank 'Thunderbolt' is part of the World War Two Memorial in the middle of the roundabout in the Place Patton in Avranches. The thunderbolt markings are similar to the ones painted on the tank commanded by U.S. Lieutenant Colonel Creighton Abrams during the liberation of Avranches on 30 July 1944. To get the American units out of the bocage country where they had incurred losses, General Bradley decided to break the enemy front at the south of Saint-Lo. The operation was codenamed *Cobra*. On 25 July 1944, 12 square kilometres of the Chapelle-en-Juger Sector experienced the largest carpet bombing in World War Two.

The VII Army Corps rushed into the breach to the south. A war of attrition and harassment made way for a war of movement. Avranches was the last barrier to cross to get to the Pontaubault Bridge. Once it was captured, it allowed General Patton's tanks to enter Brittany on 31 July 1944. Part of the force had to move east to attack German units in Mortain and Falaise.

The Place Du Général Patton was built in 1954 to honour the troops of the Third Army of General Patton whose armoured divisions completed this bold military operation: the breakthrough to Avranches. The granite pyramid measures 24m high and has five irregular and curved faces. Fifty bags of earth taken from all 50 of the United States of America were placed here.

This is one of the best-preserved Sherman tanks in Normandy. It has a coaxial machine gun sticking out of the turret gun mantlet and one in the ball mounting in the hull. There is a smoke grenade launcher present in the roof. After the war, the original Chrysler multibank engine was removed and replaced with a Continental R975 radial engine. Additional air filters were installed above the back doors, and different engine deck plates were installed that looked very similar to the engine deck plates found on the M4 and M4A1 tanks. The letter 'T' stands for 'transformé'. It was assigned to post-war French Army Sherman tanks that had these modifications.

Specifications	
Length:	6.05m
Width:	2.61m
Height:	2.74m
Weight:	31.11 tons
M4A4 Engine:	Chrysler A57 30-cylinder, 4-cycle, multibank 425hp petrol engine
M4A4T(75) Engine:	Continental R975 radial engine
Crew:	5
Main gun:	75mm gun M3 in an M34 mount
Other weapons:	Two .30cal MG M1919A4 machine guns; one .50cal MG HB M2 machine gun
Armour:	19mm–76.2mm
Sustained road speed:	25mph
Max. range on roads:	100 miles
Total M4A4 built:	7,499 (Transformé conversions total not known)

Chapter 42

Churchill Mk.VII Tank
The Battle for Hill 112 Memorial

Location: This is a difficult place to find using a navigation device. The Battle for Hill 112 Memorial is between the villages of Le Bon Repos and Éterville, which are linked by the D8. You will see the car park from the D8 crossroads with the roads called Chemin Hausse and Hill 112 Memorial. The tank is behind the line of trees.

Field Marshal Erwin Rommel is quoted as stating, 'He who controls Hill 112 controls Normandy.' It was only after soldiers from the 15th Scottish, 43rd Wessex, 53rd Welsh and 11th Armoured Divisions had finally defeated six SS Panzer Divisions in a brutal battle that lasted around ten weeks, that it was eventually captured by the Allies. It cost approximately 10,000 lives.

The memorial A22 Churchill tank is a Mk.VII armed with a 75mm gun and two 7.92mm Besa machine guns. The machine gun in the hull had a limited arc of fire due to the protruding front tracks. The second machine gun was mounted next to the main gun in the turret. This version of the Churchill tank was fitted with more armour than previous models. The armour protection ranged between 16mm and 152mm, which compared favourably to the previous models that only had armour that ranged from 16mm to 152mm. It was designed as a heavily armoured slow-moving infantry support tank and was powered by a Bedford 12-cylinder, water-cooled, horizontally opposed, L-head 350hp petrol engine. The Mk.VII Churchill only had a maximum road speed of 17.3mph (27.8km/h). It needed a crew of five: tank commander, gunner, loader/radio operator, driver, co-driver/hull machine gunner.

The memorial tank was used by the Royal Electrical and Mechanical Engineers (REME) as a tank-recovery aid at the Stanford Army Training ground (STANTA) in Thetford, Norfolk, UK. REME students would use it to learn how to recover a broken-down tank on the battlefield and how to tow a tank to the repair depot behind the front line. The tank's gun had been removed.

Sergeant Albert Figg, who served with the Royal Artillery during the struggle for Hill 112, was determined to honour his fallen colleagues at this battle. With the help of his daughter, he raised money to buy the Churchill tank as a memorial to all the tank crews who died. Carl Brown organised the recovery of the Churchill and did the cosmetic restoration with the help of Adrian Barrell. The tank is missing its track guards.

Specifications	
Length:	7.36m
Width:	2.87m
Height:	2.61m
Weight:	39.5 tons
Engine:	Bedford 12-cylinder, water-cooled, horizontally opposed, L-head 350hp petrol engine
Crew:	5
Main gun:	Royal Ordnance QF 75mm
Other weapons:	Two 7.92mm Besa machine guns
Armour:	16mm–152mm
Sustained road speed:	13.5mph (max. road speed: 17.3mph)
Max. range on roads:	142 miles

Chapter 43

M4A1(75) Sherman Grizzly Tank
Caen War Memorial

Location: Caen 14000, Avenue du Maréchal Montgomery at the junction with the Esplanade Brillaud de Laujardière, Mémorial de Caen.

The initial Allied plan was to capture the city of Caen on D-Day, but this did not happen as the Germans stubbornly defended this vital transportation hub. The Mémorial de Caen covers the origins of World War Two, the effect on civilians as well as soldiers, the development of the war around the globe, the horrors of war, the French Resistance and the Allied invasion. The tickets are expensive compared with other museums on the invasion coast. It has a surprising lack of large artefacts on display, although there is an impressive rocket-firing ground-attack RAF Typhoon in the entrance hall. There is only one tank, an M4A1 Sherman Grizzly displayed next to a Soviet BM-13 Katuska multiple rocket launcher on a ZIS-6 general-purpose lorry. The Grizzly did not see action in World War Two. They were kept in Canada as training tanks.

The Sherman Grizzly was a U.S.-designed M4A1 medium tank built in Canada by Montreal Locomotive Works after completion of the Ram II tank and Ram OP/Command contracts. It differed from the M4A1 by being fitted with Canadian CDP tracks and the installation of British wireless equipment. A stowage box was added on the turret, and sand-shields were fitted as standard.

Plans to produce the M4A1 in Canada had been made as early as September 1942. However, the limited facilities of Montreal Locomotive Works meant that production could not start for another year. Between September and December 1943, a total of 188 Canadian-built M4A1s were produced, the name Grizzly being given to this vehicle by the Canadians to differentiate it from the American-built M4A1 tanks.

Production in Canada was prematurely cut short by the decision to concentrate all Sherman tank production in American plants, which in 1944 had sufficient free production capacity to meet all M4 series tank requirements for Allied armies. The Grizzly, together with American-built M4s, equipped Canadian armoured battalions in Canada and Europe. The Portuguese Army used this tank after the war and then sold it as surplus Army stock in the 1980s to Ian McGregor of Ruthin, Wales. The museum then purchased it.

Specifications	
Length:	5.84m
Width:	2.31m
Height:	2.74m
Weight:	29.8 tons
Engine:	Continental R975 CI, 9-cylinder, 4-cycle, radial 400hp petrol engine
Crew:	5
Main gun:	75mm gun M3 in an M34 mount
Other weapons:	Two .30cal MG M1919A4 machine guns; one .50cal MG HB M2 machine gun
Armour:	12.7mm–76.2mm
Sustained road speed:	21mph
Max. range on roads:	120 miles
Total built:	188

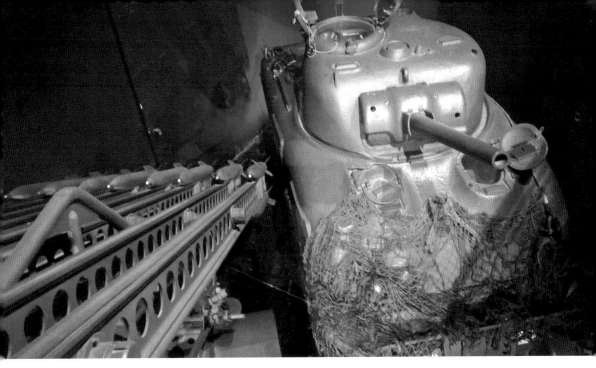

Chapter 44
M4A2(75)
Forêt d'Écouves, La Croix-de-Médavy

Location: This is a difficult location to find using a navigation device. It is in the middle of a forest at the junction of eight roads. The nearest small village is l'Etre Ragaine. At the crossroads in the village head south on the D26. Follow the signpost to Alençon and La Croix-de-Médavy. Drive for 2.5km (1.5 miles).

This M4A2(75) Sherman tank, named 'Valois', is now a memorial to the troops of the Free French 2nd Armoured Division that fought and lost their lives in the battle of the Forêt d'Écouves in August 1944. It was hit by a number of anti-tank rounds including one in the gun barrel.

In August 1944 the battle in the forest was part of the wider battle for the American-led Operation *Cobra* Falaise pocket encirclement. The 2nd French Armoured Division landed at Utah Beach on 1 August 1944 as reinforcements. They served under American General George S. Patton's Third Army. Following the recapture of Alençon on 12 August 1944, the division, led by French General Leclerc, proceeded north towards Argentan.

The armoured column entered the Forêt d'Écouves by the south in order to tackle the 9th Panzer Division, which was hidden in the forest. In Le Gateys, on the only road, a Sherman tank was hit by a German anti-tank round, resulting in the death of Colonel Rémy's 18-year-old son, Roger. At La Croix de Medavy, Shermans and Panzers clashed but the French were reinforced. The following day, on 13 August 1944, the two French armoured columns triumphed.

This particular Sherman tank was knocked out near the village of Tanville on the D226 road. At 5.45pm on Sunday 13 August 1944, a volley of shells from anti-tank guns hit the tank. The guns were hidden in the woods and belonged to the German 9th Panzer Division. Numerous German soldiers from the 5th Panzer Division had also taken refuge in the forest. By regrouping these forces, the Germans hoped to stop the Allied attempt to encircle them in the Falaise pocket.

In 1946, this war wreck was saved from being turned into scrap metal, given a new role as a war memorial and moved to its present location. The tank's hull number is 26875 and was built by the American company Fisher Body Corporation. One source says it served with the 2nd French Armoured Division (2e Division Blindée, 2e DB). Another record shows that it was part of the 3rd Squadron, 12ème Régiment de Chasseurs D'Afrique.

Specifications	
Length:	5.91m
Width:	2.61m
Height:	2.74m
Weight:	31.33 tons
Engine:	General Motors 6046 12-cylinder, 2-cycle, twin in-line, 410hp diesel engine
Crew:	5
Main gun:	75mm gun M3 in an M34A1 mount
Other weapons:	Two .30cal MG M1919A4 machine guns; one .50cal MG HB M2 machine gun; 2in mortar M3 (smoke)
Armour:	12.7mm–88.9mm
Sustained road speed:	25mph
Max. range on roads:	150 miles
Total built:	8,053

(Photographs © Pierre-Olivier Buan)

Chapter 45

M4A2(75) Sherman Tank
Écouché

Location: Écouché 61150, Avenue Léon Labbé at the junction with Rue de la 2ème DB.

This M4A2(75) Sherman tank with the name 'Massaoua' painted on the side belonged to the Free French 1st Company, 501e Régiment de Chars de Combat, 2nd Armoured Division. As part of the American-led Operation *Cobra*, this unit participated in the liberation of Écouché on 13 August 1944. A few days later, on 15 August 1944, two French Army M4A2(75) Sherman tanks called 'Massaoua' and 'Bir Hakeim' were on watch, in a defensive position on the western outskirts of the town. They were looking along the road for any Germans trying to retreat to Falaise, while other crews were carrying out maintenance on their tanks.

In the middle of the afternoon, the two tanks were spotted by some German Panzer IV medium tanks hidden from sight in a wood north-east of Écouché, on the other side of the Orne River. At a range of 800m they were able to fire the first shot. It missed and hit the ground: the second shell hit the Bir Hakeim; the third shell penetrated the ammunition compartment of the Massaouah, which caught fire. The tank commander Sergeant Major Mahaeo was thrown out of the turret. He was unscathed but later died courageously in a replacement tank named 'Massaouah II' during an attack on the town Baccarat in eastern France. The driver was not injured, but the co-driver/radio operator, Louis Léonard, who was sitting next to him, broke his foot.

The disabled tank remained in place at the entrance to the town until the end of the war. The mayor, Monsieur Chable, saved it from being cut up for scrap metal by purchasing the salvage rights for the town. It only had to be moved a few metres to its current location to enable it to be used as a memorial to all those who helped liberate this corner of French soil. In August 1947, it was officially inaugurated, In September 1952 the National Rally of veterans of the 2nd Armoured Division was held in Écouché for the first time. Annual liberation commemorative events have been held every year since that date.

Specifications	
Length:	5.91m
Width:	2.61m
Height:	2.74m
Weight:	31.33 tons
Engine:	General Motors 6046 12-cylinder, 2-cycle, twin in-line, 410hp diesel engine
Crew:	5
Main gun:	75mm gun M3 in a M34A1 mount
Other weapons:	Two .30cal MG M1919A4 machine guns; one .50cal MG HB M2 machine gun; 2in mortar M3 (smoke)
Armour:	12.7mm–88.9mm
Sustained road speed:	25mph
Max. range on roads:	150 miles
Total built:	8,053

(Photographs © Pierre-Olivier Buan)

Chapter 46

M4A2(75) Sherman Tank
D745, 1km east of Benoise

Location: This location is difficult to pinpoint using a navigation device. The nearest village is Benoise 61570. The tank is 1km east of the centre of this tiny village, in a small lay-by on the northern side of the D745 road.

This French Army M4A2(75) Sherman tank has the name 'KEREN' painted on the side. It was disabled in its current location on 12 August 1944. It remains beside the road as a memorial to its dead crew.

The tank shows significant damage, including a hole through the rear of the turret, buckling of the hull armour, and missing rubber from the tracks. It appears that following the penetration by an armour-piercing round, the ammunition detonated and the tank caught fire.

These French Army tank units were part of the American-led Operation *Cobra*. They were trying to encircle German forces in what would come to be known as the Falaise pocket. They had initially headed south from western Normandy and then turned south-east. When this tank was knocked out, its unit had changed direction again towards the north-east, trying to close the gap between the British and Commonwealth forces in the north and the U.S. forces in the south.

The M4A2(75) variant of the Sherman tank was manufactured by Fisher Body, Baldwin LW, Federal Machine and Welder, ALCO and Pullman Standard; 8,053 were produced. The protruding armoured hoods surrounding the driver's and co-driver's positions had small hatches. The engine compartment had a grilled hatch on the top to help improve ventilation, but on this tank, it has been removed and replaced with a more watertight steel plate. Unlike some other Sherman tanks, no rear engine compartment access doors were fitted. The hull armour plates were welded together. It did not have an upper hull cast metal body like some other Sherman tank variants. The turret was cast metal construction.

It was powered by a General Motors 6046 12-cylinder, 2-cycle, twin in-line, 410hp diesel engine. The Sherman would enter combat in 1942 equipped with the 75mm gun M3, a .40cal gun that could penetrate 88mm (3.5in) of unsloped rolled homogeneous armour at 100 meters (110 yards) and 73mm (2.9in) at 1,000 meters (1,100 yards) firing the usual M61 armour-piercing round. A .30cal (7.62mm) Browning M1919A4 machine gun was mounted next to the main gun in the turret. Another was fitted in a ball mount in the front glacis plate.

Specifications	
Length:	5.91m
Width:	2.61
Height:	2.74m
Weight:	31.33 tons
Engine:	General Motors 6046 12-cylinder, 2-cycle, twin in-line, 410hp diesel engine
Crew:	5
Main gun:	75mm gun M3 in an M34A1 mount
Other weapons:	Two .30cal MG M1919A4 machine guns; one .50cal (12.7mm) MG HB M2 Browning machine gun; 2in mortar M3 (smoke)
Armour:	12.7mm–88.9mm
Sustained road speed:	25mph
Max. range on roads:	150 miles
Total built:	8,053

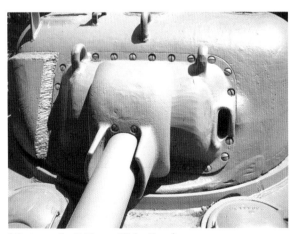

(Photographs © Pierre-Olivier Buan)

Chapter 47

M4A1(76)
Mémorial de Montormel, Les Hayettes, Montormel

Location: Mont-Ormel 61160, Les Hayettes, Mémorial de Montormel.

This M4A1(76) Sherman tank commemorates the battles fought for the liberation of France and Europe by the 1st Polish Armoured Division. On this hill, Hill 262, Mont Ormel Ridge, Polish soldiers fought a significant final action in the battle for Normandy. Between 19 and 22 August 1944 the Falaise pocket was closing. As part of the American-led Operation *Cobra* a breakthrough was forced south into France and then east with the objective of meeting up with the British and Commonwealth forces who were attacking from the north. It was hoped to encircle German forces of their 7th Army. Approximately 10,000 German troops were killed or injured; around 50,000 were captured. Vast quantities of German Army vehicles, tanks, self-propelled guns and artillery guns were either destroyed or abandoned.

As well as American troops moving up from the south, the 1st Polish Armoured Division, 2nd French Armoured Division and 4th Canadian Armoured Division took part in Operation *Cobra*. In particular, the Mémorial de Montormel commemorates the often-forgotten sacrifice of 1,441 Polish soldiers who were killed or badly injured in the field in August 1944. The 1st Polish Armoured Division suffered 2,300 casualties. Polish, Canadian and French troops also fought with the British who were attacking from the north.

On the night of 19 August 1944, having taken Chambois, soldiers from the 1st Polish Armoured Division drove north-east and established themselves on part of Hill 262, the Mont Ormel Ridge (the Mace). German General Model ordered three SS Panzer Divisions to attack the Polish position. After a very fierce battle, the attack was repulsed. From their elevated position on the ridge, they were able to call in artillery and ground attack aircraft support.

On 20 August 1944, a final German attack was launched by more SS troops. The Poles stood their ground even after having to endure close-quarters hand-to-hand combat. Just after midday, Canadian Grenadier Guards reinforcements arrived, and by late afternoon the Germans started to retreat.

The battle of the Falaise pocket ended the Battle of Normandy with a German defeat. It is estimated German casualties were around 450,000 men, of whom 240,000 were killed or wounded. Around 10,000 German troops managed to escape the encirclement.

This M4A1(76) Sherman tank, with the name 'Gen. Maczek' (Maczuga), belonged to the Polish Armoured Division. It was armed with the longer-barrelled high-velocity 76mm gun. The letter 'W' indicates that it was fitted with wet ammunition stowage bins to reduce internal fires. (For specifications, see Chapter 26.)

(Photographs © Pierre-Olivier Buan)